US Marine Infantry Combat Uniforms and Equipment 2000–2012

J. KENNETH EWARD

Series editor Martin Windrow

First published in Great Britain in 2012 by Osprey Publishing,
Midland House, West Way, Botley, Oxford, OX2 0PH, UK
44-02 23rd Street, Suite 219, Long Island City, NY 11101, USA

E-mail: info@ospreypublishing.com

OSPREY PUBLISHING IS PART OF THE OSPREY GROUP

A CIP catalog record for this book is available from the British Library

Print ISBN: 978 1 84908 799 5
PDF ebook ISBN: 978 1 84908 800 8
ePub ebook ISBN: 978 1 78096 899 5

Editor: Martin Windrow
Index by Rob Munro
Typeset in Sabon and Myriad Pro
Originated by PDQ Digital Medi, Bungay, UK
Printed in China through Worldprint Ltd.

12 13 14 15 16 10 9 8 7 6 5 4 3 2 1

Osprey Publishing is supporting the Woodland Trust, the UK's leading woodland conservation charity, by funding the dedication of trees.

www.ospreypublishing.com

ACKNOWLEDGEMENTS

A book on a contemporary topic such as this cannot rely entirely on written documents, but also rests on the efforts of a great number of knowledgeable people. I am grateful for the assistance of the United States Marine Corps and of many individuals during the writing of the manuscript. In particular, I wish to thank Maj C.B. Redding, Media Branch Head of USMC Public Affairs, and other PA personnel for their help throughout the project: Capts Joshua Diddams and Kevin H. Schultz, 1st Lt Jamie Larson and MGySgt Mark Oliva. The Marine Corps History Division also gave unstintingly of their knowledge, and I thank Senior Editor Kenneth H. Williams, Annette Amerman, Vincent J. Martinez and Cynthia M. Meyer for their kind help in locating older materials. Numerous others also gave generously: Sgt Nicholas H. Freisthler, Guy A. Haskins, Casey McKether, LCpl Christopher E. Kelty, 1st Sgt Harry H. Kindrick, Adam Lauritson, MSgt Maceo W. Mathis II, and Cpl Joshua A. Sochanek. Thanks are owed also to Dahl Studio and especially to my wife, Rosemary Marusak, for her help and support throughout this project. Lastly, I'd like to thank my editor, Martin Windrow, who planted the seeds of this book long ago. To all, I wish to express my heartfelt thanks and appreciation.

AUTHOR'S NOTE

This book is a survey of general-issue combat clothing and equipment used by infantry and most other dismounted Marines; it is not encyclopedic, nor does it include equipment developed for special operations units or combat vehicle crews (which would fill books in their own right). Where multiple names exist for a single piece of equipment, the most common or most descriptive term is used here. The names of specific items of equipment are capitalized if the item is normally referred to by an acronym – e.g., Individual First Aid Kit (IFAK) – but are otherwise left uncapitalized.

A word about USMC **acronyms**: much of the language of the Marine Corps – its nouns and verbs – consists of acronyms. Indeed, these are not generally spelled out, but pronounced – and thought of – as words. In this book casual use of acronyms has been kept to a minimum wherever practical, and a **glossary** has been provided to make the text more accessible to newcomers to the subject (**see page 63**); but acronyms are unavoidable when discussing modern military equipment, and a large number will inevitably be encountered in this text.

Finally, a word about identifying USMC formations: In Marine Corps parlance, an infantry regiment is usually referred to simply by its ordinal number (e.g. "Sixth Marines"). The shorthand for a Marine battalion is written as its number, slash, and the number of its parent regiment. Thus, the 1st Battalion, 6th Infantry Regiment becomes "1/6 Marines". This notation is especially convenient when identifying personnel of a Marine Expeditionary Unit, who serve on a rotating basis.

CONTENTS

INTRODUCTION   4
Organization • "Corporate identity"

INFANTRY COMBAT EQUIPMENT DESIGN   8
Research, development, procurement and refinement • What a Marine carries, and where it comes from

COMBAT CLOTHING   12
Camouflage patterns and equipment colors • Utility uniforms • Footwear • Flame-resistant clothing • Extended Cold Weather Clothing System • All-Purpose Environmental Clothing System • Mountain/ Cold Weather Clothing System • Combat Desert Jacket • Insignia and badges

PERSONAL PROTECTIVE EQUIPMENT   26
Body armor: Interceptor OTV – SAPI plates – attachments and enhancements – Modular Tactical Vest – Scalable Plate Carrier – IMTV and PC – PPS • Helmets: PASGT – LWH – NPP attachment – contingency use of ACH – ECH • Joint protection • Eye protection • Hearing protection • Chemical, Biological, Radiological and Nuclear protective equipment

LOAD-CARRYING EQUIPMENT   38
Integrated Individual Fighting System • Modular Lightweight Load-carrying Equipment • MOLLE II and "USMC MOLLE" • Improved Load-Bearing Equipment • Family of ILBE • Other load-carrying equipment

BIVOUAC & SPECIAL-PURPOSE ITEMS   46
Tarpaulin and poncho liner • 3-Season Sleep System • Mechanical Breacher's Kit • Cold Weather Infantry Kit • Assault Climber's Kit • Sensors • Observation and illumination: binoculars – night vision equipment – flashlights • Communication equipment

INFANTRY WEAPONS   51
Bayonets and fighting knives • Pistols, rifles, carbines and shotguns • Sniper and designated marksman rifles • Squad automatic weapons and machine guns • Small-arms sights and target illuminators • Grenades and grenade launchers • Anti-personnel explosives • Rocket launchers • Mortars • Non-lethal weapons

FUTURE DEVELOPMENTS   62

GLOSSARY OF ACRONYMS   63

INDEX   64

US MARINE CORPS INFANTRY COMBAT CLOTHING & EQUIPMENT 2000–2012

INTRODUCTION

In April 2000, Marines of the 15th Marine Expeditionary Unit landed on a Kuwaiti beach just south of the Iraqi border in support of Operation *Eager Mace*. This landing was not a raid, but part of a joint exercise with Kuwaiti troops, held annually since the 1991 Gulf War for the purpose of deterring Iraqi adventurism. Although these Marines could not have known it at the time, American combat forces would spend the next decade fighting in the Middle East and Southwest Asia. The 15th MEU would itself spearhead this effort the following year, as it established a forward operating base in Afghanistan with the assistance of Navy SEALs. The "Long War" – as the American- and British-led military interventions in Afghanistan and Iraq came to be known – defined the planning of the US armed services for a generation, reshaping tactical doctrine and even equipment design.

The United States Marine Corps has played a prominent part in these conflicts from their beginnings. Collectively, they have become the longest sustained military action in Corps history. As the character of these conflicts changed from lightning invasion to grueling, drawn-out occupation, the USMC found its resources stretched far beyond the normal limits – eventually, one of every two Marine battalions would be committed to a combat theater at any given time – yet it still managed to maintain preparedness for its primary role as a conventional amphibious shock force, and to pursue vigorous programs to refine its training, tactics and matériel.

When the collapse of the Soviet regime brought the Cold War to a close in 1991, the US embarked on a period of steep cuts in military personnel and spending. Base closures – particularly of overseas facilities – were common, and investment in research and development (R&D) was pruned back. However, Marine Corps leaders saw these years of relative austerity as a time of increased national need for the USMC and its specialization in rapid deployment, peacekeeping and humanitarian relief. With the ability to quickly respond to

Captured in a moment emblematic of their history and doctrine, US Marines "hit the beach" during a 2010 exercise in Thailand. Despite the severe constraints imposed by a decade of operations in Iraq and Afghanistan, the USMC remains engaged in commitments around the globe. It participates in conventional exercises, deploys to regional hotspots, and provides humanitarian relief missions in the wake of natural disasters. (Staff Sgt Leo A. Salinas/USMC)

An antitank assault team of the 3rd Battalion, 6th Marine Regiment during a deployment that demands very different skills from their official specialty. Led by an NCO armed with a 12-gauge shotgun, they are searching for insurgents during Operation *Steel Curtain*, a November 2005 mission in northwestern Iraq near the Syrian border. (Sgt Jerad W. Alexander/USMC)

a crisis by one of its seaborne expeditionary forces continuously deployed around the globe, the Marine Corps could maintain a global US military presence even in the absence of permanent bases. Strategists reasoned that this capability would be particularly important in years to come, as the threat of local and regional destabilizations around the world eclipsed that of a major nuclear or conventional war. It was with this perspective that the USMC entered the 21st century.

Marine involvement in the invasion of Afghanistan began in November 2001, with the seizure of Camp Rhino by seaborne helicopter assault and the subsequent capture of Kandahar International Airport. The total USMC commitment in support of Coalition operations was small at this stage of the war, never rising above (light) brigade strength. The outcome was a great success, validating the Marines' brand of maneuver warfare; yet a number of important lessons were learned, including the need for better small-unit communications, and improved coordination of combined arms.

Large-scale combat deployment of Marines began during the March 2003 Coalition invasion of Iraq, in which the 1st Marine Expeditionary Force and US Army 3d Infantry Division struck out from Kuwait in a pincers movement to envelop Baghdad, fighting a series of sharp battles and skirmishes along the way. The 1st MEF also supported British forces in the capture of the southeastern port of Basrah and surrounding oilfields. By early May organized resistance had ended – only to be replaced by an insurgency movement that the Marines would battle in their assigned occupation zone of Anbar Province for the remainder of their time in Iraq. Through a combination of aggressive actions against guerrillas and goodwill gestures toward civilians, the Marines succeeded in quelling much of the violence in their area of responsibility following a troop surge in 2007.

The experience severely tested the resources of the Marine Corps: matériel was drawn from strategic reserves, and often left in theater to be shared between rotating units. The shortage in personnel was so acute that participation in the 2007 surge was accomplished largely by extending the deployment cycles of Marines stationed in Iraq rather than by adding new personnel. The USMC combat mission to Iraq ended in January 2010, in advance of a 2011 Coalition withdrawal as military authority was turned over to the new Iraqi government. Marines were then sent to reinforce Coalition troops in Afghanistan, where they took up residence in the Taliban heartland of Helmand Province and neighboring areas to resume counterinsurgency operations. A reduction in the Marine presence in Afghanistan is planned for late 2012, in preparation for a scheduled general exit of Coalition combat forces by 2014.

Events in Iraq and Afghanistan over the past decade have come to dominate the Marine Corps experience in a way that no conflict has since the Vietnam War, but this is not the whole story. During this time the USMC has maintained – albeit at a much reduced level – an engagement in international training exercises, humanitarian relief, counter-narcotics and smaller armed conflicts around the world: in Norway, the Philippines, the Horn of Africa, Turkey, Bosnia, Louisiana and Mississippi in the United States, Indonesia and Egypt, to name but a few. With the end of the "Long War" in view, the USMC plans a return to its pre-war focus on amphibious maneuver and an increased investment in training, despite the period of budgetary retrenchment that is certain to follow.

Organization

The US Marine Corps is structured as a rapid-deployment expeditionary force. Its expertise in amphibious operations, forward-deployment of forces on continuous rotation, and strategic prepositioning of supplies have made it an organization ideally suited to respond to regional crises around the globe, both as a combat force and as a provider of humanitarian relief – often as both.

The fundamental unit of organization for USMC combat strike forces is the Marine Air-Ground Task Force (MAGTF). The MAGTF can be scaled in size to meet the task at hand, and consists of command, ground, aviation and logistics components. Currently the USMC has three primary standing MAGTFs, each centering on one of its three Marine Expeditionary Forces (MEFs). Each MEF is assigned to the command of either Marine Corps Forces Atlantic or Pacific, and is composed of a reinforced infantry division, air wing and combat logistics group (see diagram). The combat arm of the Marine Corps also includes reserve and, since 2006, special operations forces, whose personnel may provide support to a MAGTF. Smaller MAGTFs may be created from the host MEF, which acts as a reservoir of manpower. These

Simplified organizational diagram of USMC combat forces. (Author)

USMC COMBAT FORCES

Marine Corps Forces Cmd. (Atlantic) — Marine Corps Forces, Pacific — Marine Corps Forces, Reserve — Special Operations Cmd.

II MEF — I MEF — III MEF

MEF (typical)

HQ Grp. — Marine Division — Marine Air Wing — Marine Logistics Grp.

MEB Cmd. Element

MEU

MAGTFs include the Marine Expeditionary Brigade (MEB) and Marine Expeditionary Unit (MEU).

The Marine Expeditionary Brigade is not a standing brigade, but is a notional force only, to be staffed by personnel drawn from the host MEF if a contingency arises. The Marine Expeditionary Unit, on the other hand, is a standing battalion-size force whose personnel are drawn from the host MEF on a rotating basis. MEUs are embarked on amphibious ready groups able to respond to emergencies and for special operations – for this reason they are usually designated MEU(SOC), for 'special operations-capable'. Typically, three MEUs are drawn from each MEF and go to sea in rotation. Like their host MEF, the smaller MEB and MEU types of MAGTF comprise command, ground, air and logistics components. A fourth type of MAGTF also exists: the Special-Purpose MAGTF. This is not a standing MAGTF, but is organized to carry out specific combat operations, training exercises and other tasks.

"Corporate identity"

The US Marine Corps fought an existential battle with other branches of the American military services throughout much of its earlier history. Because its military capabilities overlapped those of the Army, the USMC looked to define a unique mission in order to preserve its existence as an independent armed service, ultimately cementing a reputation as an elite amphibious rapid deployment force in the years leading up to and during World War II.

In this pursuit, the USMC has succeeded in cultivating a "corporate identity" of its own, one that is distinct in customs, attire and even combat equipment. The passage of time has done nothing to dull this institutional sense of identity – indeed, Marines have worked unceasingly to hone it. A

The Marine Corps is more conscious of its "brand" than most fighting forces. This label, from an article of flame-resistant clothing, would not look out of place in a retail clothing store. (Author's photo)

symbol of this identity is the Eagle, Globe and Anchor emblem (EGA), used in various forms since the mid 19th century. The EGA has since been trademarked, achieving status as a commercial logo as well as an institutional symbol. During its history, the EGA has been incorporated into a range of insignia and used to brand utility uniforms, boots and a variety of other equipment – it has even been integrated into the very design of the current MARPAT camouflage patterns used for clothing and individual equipment, which have accumulated a number of additional Marine-specific markings over the years. In addition to the increased level of "branding," a savvy design consciousness has arisen in recent years, driven by institutional pride and the need to attract new recruits – even clothing labels have received a makeover.

INFANTRY COMBAT EQUIPMENT DESIGN

The old military admonition, "Remember that your weapon was made by the lowest bidder," while holding a kernel of truth, implies certain assumptions that are not necessarily true. In the case of the modern Marine Corps and the US military as a whole, the value attached to human life has never been greater, nor has the premium attached to protecting it. In light of the considerable effort made to provide equipment that safeguards that life, another truism – "You get what you pay for" – may be more appropriate. The cost to outfit a Marine is $8,000 (at 2011 prices). This cost, which does not include electronic communication or targeting devices, has risen dramatically over the past decade, and largely reflects a greater investment in protective equipment constructed of advanced materials. Wartime budget increases have made possible an intensive R&D effort and the replacement of worn-out or obsolescent equipment with new designs. At the same time, the inevitable teething problems that accompany accelerated R&D cycles have served to hasten the obsolescence of even newly-designed equipment, begetting replacement by yet newer designs.

A key trend in infantry combat equipment design during the past decade has been toward increasing the modularity of systems – the ability to reconfigure equipment to meet changing mission requirements. Modularity has featured in nearly every aspect of a Marine infantryman's gear, including body armor, load-carrying equipment and even weaponry. Improved protection and ergonomics is another consistent theme in the design of infantry clothing and equipment. Examples include the introduction of flame-resistant garments and bullet-resistant body armor for Marine ground forces, the use of lighter-weight, less bulky materials, and the fielding of load-carrying equipment designed to minimize fatigue. Improvements in

A mortarman of the 1/2 Marines adjusts the sight of his 60mm mortar during a 2007 Military Operations in Urban Terrain (MOUT) training exercise. Note on the rear suspension pad of his Lightweight Helmet the familiar Eagle, Globe & Anchor emblem. The use of "trademarks" and uniform ornamentation have increased in recent years, not so much reflecting a change in Corps culture as an affirmation of pride in service. (Lance Cpl Scott Schmidt/USMC)

ergonomics and weight reduction, recognized in the 2007 Marine Corps Science & Technology Strategic Plan, have become especially important in the light of another trend: the burgeoning load carried by a typical Marine in recent years, resulting largely from an increased reliance on body armor. A final trend has been a greater use of communications, target acquisition and sensing devices.

Because Marine Corps ground forces share similar needs with Army troops but fall under the jurisdiction of the Navy, they benefit from the research and development efforts of both organizations. The USMC and Army collaborate on the development of new infantry equipment at the Army's Soldier Research, Development & Engineering Center in Natick, Massachusetts, which is where most infantry equipment is designed. Additional research efforts are carried out through the Office of Naval Research (ONR) and the Defense Advanced Research Projects Agency (DARPA).

Development and procurement of combat equipment have become particularly challenging in recent years with the need to equip Marines for both conventional and unconventional warfare. Marine Corps Combat Development Command (MCCDC) is tasked broadly with developing USMC combat capabilities, including material development. Specific oversight of infantry equipment planning, development and procurement is carried out by Marine Corps Systems Command (MCSC). Since 2005, its efforts have focused on equipping infantry personnel, drawing on lessons learned from recent combat experience. MCSC keeps track of how well equipment performs in the field, encouraging feedback from deployed forces. Also, when a Marine is injured or killed, his or her equipment is analyzed by MCSC technicians for possible material or design flaws, and the results used to guide future improvements.

A number of subordinate departments help ensure that Marines receive equipment best meeting their needs. One such unit is the Marine Enhancement

A gunnery sergeant on patrol in Afghanistan; note the dark metal rank insignia pinned to his left sleeve pocket – one solution to the problem of displaying rank while wearing collared body armor.
He has expended an unusual degree of artistic effort in personalizing his LAW rocket launcher, an essentially disposable weapon. (Sgt Mark Fayloga/USMC)

Program (MEP), initiated in 1989. The MEP is a streamlined program empowered to quickly adapt "commercial off-the-shelf" (COTS) items of equipment in response to needs expressed by Marines in the field. In this way, the lengthy development and contract solicitation process can be bypassed to meet certain exigencies. MEP has been particularly active following the invasions of Afghanistan and Iraq, procuring equipment badly needed by deployed Marines. Examples include specific items of flame-resistant combat clothing, weapons and accessories, communications gear, load-carrying equipment, head and eye protection and many other items.

Marines of the 1st Bn, 1st Regt conducting a live-fire training exercise in Kuwait. For a short time in early 2005 the 1/1 carried out the unusual practice (for Marines) of wearing recognition markings on their uniforms and helmet covers. These were in the shape of triangles, fashioned in a variety of sizes and from a variety of materials, including IR-reflective plastic. (Lance Cpl Thomas J. Grove/USMC).

Another organization, the Marine Corps Warfighting Laboratory, is a MCCDC department established in 1995 to study tactical concerns. It contributes to the planning of new infantry equipment from the perspective of tactical utility. A recent addition is the Marine Expeditionary Rifle Squad (MERS) program Gruntworks facility, founded in 2007. Gruntworks is tasked with the integration of infantry combat equipment developed in different design programs, ensuring that protective equipment, load-carrying equipment, weaponry, and other gear will work well as an ensemble and that incompatibilities do not develop. An outline of how the USMC should use these assets to capitalize on innovation and advanced technology in the 21st century is codified in *Marine Corps Strategy 21*, a document written in support of the inter-service *Joint Vision 2020* strategic blueprint for the near-term future of the US military.

A NEW EQUIPMENT FOR THE NEW MILLENIUM

The US Marine Corps entered the 21st century with a mélange of load-bearing equipment on its hands. The Modular Lightweight Load-Carrying Equipment (MOLLE) system had recently been introduced in large numbers, but had not entirely displaced its predecessors, the All-purpose Lightweight Carrying Equipment (ALICE) and Integrated Individual Fighting System (IIFS). Both IIFS and ALICE persisted in infantry units as late as 2001, and were used by support units and recruits in training for several more years.

1: Major, Marine Corps Air-Ground Combat Center, early 2000

While on a combined-arms exercise in the training area around Twentynine Palms, California, this officer wears the standard three-color desert camouflage utility uniform that had replaced the six-color "chocolate chip" pattern two years previously. His IIFS load-bearing equipment marks a departure from the traditional method of suspending infantry equipment from a waist belt (as typified by ALICE), moving many items to the torso for better weight distribution and to make room for additional equipment if needed. He is armed with a Beretta M9 service pistol.

2: Machine gunner, 3rd Marine Infantry Regiment, February 2001

He wears the uniform and equipment characteristic of the late 20th century: Woodland camouflage utilities; Personnel Armor System, Ground Troops (PASGT) "flak vest" and helmet; and ALICE load-carrying equipment. Of particular interest is the night-vision goggle mount on his helmet: nighttime maneuvers were an emerging feature of US tactical doctrine, aided by increasingly capable technology. He is armed with the M240 medium machine gun fitted with a muzzle attachment for firing blanks, and an M9 pistol.

3: Hospital Corpsman; Exercise *Tandem Thrust*, Australia, 2001

The concept of a distributed load introduced in the IIFS system was continued in the next-generation Modular Lightweight Load-Carrying Equipment. This MOLLE Load-Bearing Vest (LBV) is an early item issued with two types of interchangeable waist belts (later consolidated in the MOLLE II Fighting Load Carrier). The MOLLE system was intended to be issued in several configurations, each optimized for a different combat role. Kits were configured for riflemen, automatic riflemen equipped with the M249, grenadiers, and personnel authorized to carry a pistol. A medical pack and detachable pouches (issued in sets of eight) were made specifically for medical personnel. This corpsman is checking his medical pack.

What a Marine carries, and where it comes from

On entering Boot Camp, a recruit receives basic uniform articles, physical training gear, toiletries and other personal items, collectively referred to as "sea bag" items. A Marine recruit will carry these throughout his or her career – or at least until they are worn out and replaced. The recruit also receives Infantry Combat Equipment (ICE) with which to train. Traditionally called "deuce gear" or "782 gear" (after the Form 782 on which equipment was once signed for), these items include body armor, load-carrying equipment and other gear, and are returned upon graduation. Equipment issued for recruit training typically consists of older models no longer in use with active units; in this way the useful lifetime of equipment is extended.

Upon graduation from recruit training and assignment to a unit, the newly-minted Marine draws combat equipment from the local Individual Issue Facility (IIF), which is still usually referred to as CIF, for the now-defunct Consolidated Issue Facility it recently replaced. Each unit maintains its own inventory of this organizational (in contrast to personal) equipment, which is used by its Marines until their transfer to a new post or retirement. Additional, specialized equipment may be requisitioned from a Special Training Allowance Pool (STAP) upon a unit's deployment. This equipment is intended for limited-term use during the period of deployment, and typically includes hot or cold weather clothing and equipment, flame-resistant protective gear, and many other items. The Special Training Allowance Pool is now managed by the Unit Issue Facility (UIF) network, as is Chemical, Biological, Radiological & Nuclear (CBRN) protective garb and testing equipment. The modern Marine accumulates a considerable amount of combat equipment in preparation for deployment, designed to carry heavy loads; a Marine's full marching load of equipment and provisions can easily top 135lb in weight. Even a comparatively light combat load can total 80–90lb when body armor, load-carrying equipment, rifle, ammunition, rations, water and other supplies are factored in.

Many replacement uniform items may be purchased by the Marine from vendors approved through the USMC Vendor Certification Program.

A supply clerk inspects the body armor of 11th MEU Marines – male and female – prior to their deployment to the Western Pacific. In addition to basic items drawn during recruit training, Marines are issued infantry combat equipment at the time they join a permanent unit, and may receive additional equipment prior to a deployment, subject to their commander's discretion. These Marines wear utilities and the famous "eight-point cover" in Woodland MARPAT camouflage pattern. (Cpl Chad J. Pulliam/USMC)

Marines may also purchase certain commercial models of combat equipment privately, or receive commercial equipment from their commanders, who have purchased it with discretionary funds to fill an immediate need. This was particularly common at the beginning of the war in Iraq, when there were shortages of certain items, but it is now usually a matter of personal preference rather than need. After receiving reports of avoidable injuries received as the result of commercial equipment that did not meet protective standards, the USMC has drawn up lists of approved commercial alternatives to many issue items; these have been tested to ensure they provide an equivalent level of quality and/or protection to the issue item.

COMBAT CLOTHING

Camouflage patterns and equipment colors

At the beginning of the millennium the familiar Woodland camouflage scheme, with its distinctive whorls of subdued hues, remained the standard US temperate zone camouflage pattern for textiles used in combat clothing and equipment. This pattern had been in use by all armed services since its introduction in the early 1980s. The standard joint-service desert camouflage, a three-tone pattern, had been adopted in the late 1990s by the USMC. It

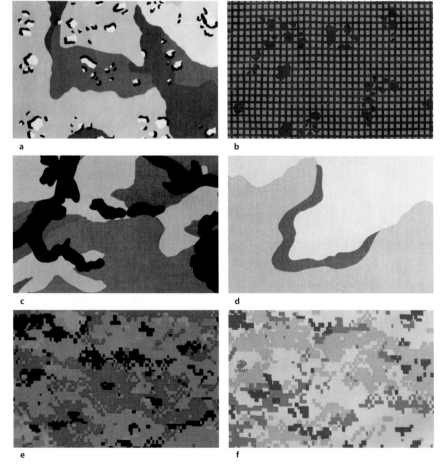

(a & b) These two camouflage patterns – the six-color "chocolate chip" desert day camouflage, and its nighttime equivalent – became obsolete in the late 1990s, but saw limited continuing use into the 21st century, albeit predominantly in a training role. The following swatches, shown to scale, illustrate camouflage fabrics used in USMC uniforms and personal equipment during the first years of the 21st century. (c & d) Woodland pattern, and three-color desert camouflage. Although replaced by MARPAT early on, they persisted in service for many years – in CBRN suits and other items of stockpiled equipment. (e & f) Woodland MARPAT camouflage, and Desert MARPAT. The sharp-eyed will be able to make out the shape of the USMC's Eagle, Globe and Anchor "logo" actually worked into the design of these patterns. (Author's photos) replaced the Gulf War-era six-tone daytime desert camouflage pattern – informally called "chocolate chip," from its fancied resemblance to the quintessential American cookie. The six-tone daytime camouflage was issued with a complementary nighttime pattern, produced with infrared-absorbent dyes designed to evade detection by enemy personnel equipped with night vision devices. Unlike the older six-tone daytime pattern, the new three-tone desert camouflage used dyes that extended its effectiveness into the infrared spectrum, so could be used day or night. The transition to the new desert camouflage occurred over a period of years, and it was still possible to see articles of clothing in the older patterns during the post-2003 occupation of Iraq – even after the new three-color pattern had itself been replaced.

With an eye toward developing a new field uniform, the Marine Corps made plans at the turn of the millennium to develop new camouflage patterns unique to its service. It initiated a study of existing camouflage schemes worldwide, and was particularly impressed by tests of a so-called "digital" pattern developed by Canada in the 1990s (CADPAT). Reminiscent of tiled mosaic, digital camouflage designs had their origins in World War II; but while early patterns used by Soviet troops in 1944 were designed by hand, CADPAT was engineered with the assistance of modern computer-aided design. Working in cooperation with Canadian Armed Forces, the USMC produced a new scheme that it called Marine Pattern, or MARPAT for short. In its appearance, MARPAT is a disruptive mosaic pattern derived from a banded, tiger-stripe motif. Its patterns are repeated at multiple scales to

B **MODULAR LIGHTWEIGHT LOAD-CARRYING EQUIPMENT**

The MOLLE system improved on IIFS by affording flexibility in the placement of equipment pouches, which could be positioned at the wearer's discretion. At the heart of the early MOLLE system was the Load-Bearing Vest (LBV), which was combined with a waist belt to create a platform for attaching pouches.

An arrangement typical for an M249 gunner is shown in (1). This includes a hand grenade pouch fixed to the upper left side webbing of the LBV, and several items of equipment attached to the utility belt, including (from left to right) a 200-round M249 pouch; a 1-quart canteen in an ALICE carrier; a MOLLE butt pack with individual first aid pouch attached; a second canteen; and a 100-round M249 pouch, which doubled as a general-purpose utility pouch. The early MOLLE system did not feature a new canteen carrier or updated first aid kit, so existing ALICE items were retained until replacements were developed. Because ALICE attachment clips are incompatible with the MOLLE Pouch Attachment Ladder System, adapters (2) were provided. Additional MOLLE pouches were provided for carrying a 15-round 9mm pistol magazine (3), a single 30-round M16 magazine (4) or two magazines (5). The 3-liter "Storm" hydration system (6) was intended as a supplement to the two canteens.

The early LBV could be attached to either the MOLLE utility belt (shown in 1) for light fighting load orders, or to a molded waist belt (7) for use with the main pack. The molded belt featured a socket connector designed to take a corresponding probe on the pack frame; in this way the pack could theoretically be carried securely but disengaged quickly.

Because the pack had a tendency to bounce loose from the socket, this design was abandoned in the MOLLE II specification. The molded waist belt became a permanent fixture of the pack frame, and the LBV and utility belt were combined into a new pattern of load-carrying vest.

The MOLLE pack system included a main pack and sleep-system carrier on a pack frame; a patrol pack, worn for shorter missions; and two sustainment pouches that could add additional capacity. The latter were usually attached to either side of the main pack, but could also be used with the patrol pack. Several configurations of the pack system were possible, accommodating a range of loads. The full rucksack load (8) comprised the main pack above the sleep-system carrier, both secured to the plastic pack frame; a sustainment pouch fixed each side of the main pack; and a patrol pack carried "piggyback" on top of everything else. The butt pack could also be worn simultaneously, provided that the utility belt was worn with the LBV and the molded waist belt was semi-permanently strapped to the pack frame; its normal position was hanging suspended from the utility belt, riding below the sleep-system carrier.

The pack system included a SINCGARS pouch for radio operators (9), which was normally fastened inside the main pack but could also be carried separately on a general-purpose strap; and a bandolier for six additional M16 magazines (10). The final component of the system was a pair of 6ft lashing straps (11) for securing additional cargo. Most features of the pack system remained unchanged in MOLLE II; an exception was a new patrol pack (12) which featured several improvements, including a 25 percent increase in cargo capacity.

The Snow MARPAT camouflage has a blotchier appearance when compared to the banded design of its temperate and desert equivalents, and the individual elements are larger. (Author)

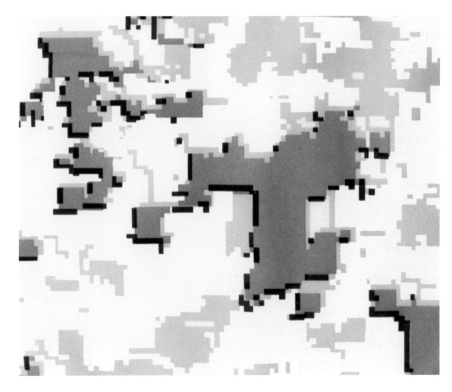

The Snow MARPAT camouflage has a blotchier appearance when compared to the banded design of its temperate and desert equivalents, and the individual elements are larger. (Author)

improve effectiveness at close range as well as providing concealment at the longer ranges for which the older Woodland camouflage had been designed. In addition to the pattern developed for temperate climates, called Woodland MARPAT, desert and snow versions were also created. Desert MARPAT is similar stylistically to its temperate zone cousin, differing chiefly in the colors used; Snow MARPAT has a somewhat blotchy rather than banded appearance, and is printed at a larger scale, but shares the same origins. The new patterns feature the Marine Corps Eagle, Globe & Anchor logo integrated into the design – a measure intended to discourage commercial copying – and made their appearance in 2002. Despite the conversion to MARPAT and its exclusive use on newer items of clothing and equipment, the older Woodland and desert camouflage patterns continue in service even today as existing stocks of load-bearing and protective articles are used up. Not uncommonly, especially during the early years of the war in Iraq, Marines could be seen wearing several patterns simultaneously.

To complement the new MARPAT camouflage schemes, a new ground color was chosen to replace the olive drab traditionally used in American load-carrying equipment. Called Coyote Brown 498, this color is a drab brown, somewhat darker than the golden-khaki used in USMC web equipment in the early 20th century. Coyote brown first began to appear on body armor in 2003, then on other items of load-bearing equipment. All textile components of Marine Corps field equipment are now produced in either MARPAT or a solid coyote brown.

A final camouflage pattern must also be mentioned: Multi-Terrain Pattern, the current British Ministry of Defence camouflage pattern for uniforms and personal equipment. MTP is a hybrid pattern combining features of British Disruptive Pattern Material (DPM) and MultiCam, a commercially-developed pattern in use with the US Army and Marine Corps

Special Operations Command. MTP is not an official USMC pattern, but appears on British pelvic body armor adopted in 2011 to fill an Urgent Universal Need Statement for Marines deployed to Afghanistan.

Utility uniforms

Marines in the year 2000 had for nearly 20 years worn the Battle Dress Uniform in common with the Army and other services. Called the BDU by the other services, this uniform was known by Marines as the "combat utility uniform" or "cammies." The coat featured four bellows pockets and reinforced elbows; the trousers featured large side cargo pockets, knee and seat reinforcement, and ankle drawstring adjustment. The combat utility uniform was manufactured in both Woodland and desert camouflage (in both six- and three-tone patterns), and midweight and lightweight versions broadened its suitability across a wide range of environments.

A new two-piece Marine Corps Combat Utility Uniform (MCCUU) was introduced as a replacement in 2002. Better known as "MARPATs" for the new camouflage pattern it bore, the new uniform featured several changes from the old style. The two hip pockets of the coat – normally covered by combat equipment, and thus of marginal use – were eliminated; the breast pockets were canted for improved access, and sleeve pockets were also added. In later production, Velcro patches were added to the sleeve pocket flaps for attachment of infrared-reflective recognition tabs for night operations. The EGA emblem was no longer an iron-on appliqué, but embroidered on the left breast pocket. The new trousers featured elastic at the waistband and side cargo pockets, while ankle drawstrings were eliminated. A new feature of the MCCUU was the incorporation of internal pockets to hold removable foam polymer elbow and knee pads. The new uniform was manufactured in a midweight nylon/cotton twill in both Woodland MARPAT and Desert MARPAT versions. As with the earlier uniform, some MCCUUs were factory-impregnated with Permethrin insect repellent.

The distinctive USMC garrison cover (USMC parlance for a cap) – commonly known as the "eight-point cover" for its shape – has been in continuous use since its adoption in World War II, becoming closely tied to Corps tradition. This cap is produced in MARPAT for the new uniform, as is the broad-brimmed, floppy field cover or "boonie." Both caps are embroidered with the EGA. An olive green T-shirt is worn with the utility uniform. Initially produced in cotton, the shirt began to be issued in 2003 in both cotton and synthetic versions. A 2006 order in response to mounting numbers of burn casualties in Iraq resulted in the development of a new flame-resistant undershirt (see below, "Flame-resistant clothing"). The nylon web belt worn with the MCCUU reflects the wearer's prowess in unarmed combat. Following the establishment of the Marine Martial Arts Program in 2001, Marines no longer wear a standard belt, but instead a Martial Arts Utility Belt in a color corresponding to their martial arts rank. Colors range from tan (proficiency earned in basic training) through gray, green, brown, and six progressive degrees of black belt.

Footwear

In the late 1990s, Marines were issued no fewer than three kinds of temperate and warm weather boots: the standard black leather combat boot, a jungle boot, and a desert boot, the latter two with textile uppers. The Corps sought to develop an updated combat boot, taking advantage of newer materials and more sophisticated ergonomics. The result was the Marine Corps Combat Boot (MCCB), which was designed in two versions: one with a Gore-Tex water barrier for temperate-climate use, the other featuring ventilation grommets and optimized for hot climates. Although the MCCB represented a great improvement over previous designs, and simplified logistics, the Marine Corps identified areas for improvement – particularly with regard to durability in rocky and mountainous areas – and began work on a successor to the MCCB: the Rugged All-Terrain (RAT) boot, which began field testing in 2009. The RAT features additional toe and heel reinforcement caps for greater abrasion resistance, an especially important concern in rocky and icy mountainous areas. Like the MCCB before it, the RAT is produced in both temperate and hot-weather versions.

Flame-resistant clothing (FROG)

An increase in the occurrence of burn injuries, stemming from the intensified use of improvised explosive devices (IEDs) by insurgents in Iraq, led to a 2006 requirement for flame-resistant (FR) clothing on combat missions and at forward operating bases in Iraq – and later Afghanistan. Utility uniforms and other garments containing synthetic fibers, while still worn on base, were no longer permitted "outside the wire." To fill the immediate needs of the 33,000 Marines then stationed in Iraq's Al Anbar province, infantry units at forward bases were issued flame-resistant Nomex flight and vehicle crew coveralls and gloves until infantry-specific uniforms could be developed. The new infantry flame-resistant ensemble, termed Flame-Resistant Organizational Gear (FROG), began production in December 2006 after an accelerated development cycle, and began to be issued to Marines in Iraq shortly afterward. The FROG designation is also applied to other types of flame-resistant combat clothing, including the flame-resistant aviator and vehicle clothing temporarily in use with dismounted infantry.

The FROG ensemble consists of several garments intended to cover as much of the body as possible. A long-sleeve T-shirt is worn with an outer

---

C | MOLLE & INTERCEPTOR BODY ARMOR

The Interceptor Outer Tactical Vest (OTV) and SAPI armor plates (1) replaced the PASGT vest. The OTV shares the pouch attachment system of the MOLLE load-bearing vests (LBV and FLC), and can either be worn underneath the vest or instead of it, by direct attachment of pouches. The front flap of this example is open, revealing the compartment holding the front SAPI plate. The rear SAPI plate (shown behind the vest) is held in a similar compartment in back. An improved Individual First Aid Kit (IFAK) and KA-BAR combat knife with MOLLE adapter (2) are attached.

3: Squad leader, Task Force Tarawa; advance on Baghdad, March 2003

With his helmet knocked askew, he wears the Saratoga CBRN protective suit and carries protective gloves, overboots and M40 gasmask (4) at the ready. He has mounted his equipment directly on his OTV, and holds an M16A2 rifle fitted with the M203 40mm grenade launcher.

The MOLLE 40mm grenade pouches include one holding two pyrotechnic rounds (5) – here, an example in the new "coyote brown" color – and pouches for HE rounds in pairs (6) or

singly (7). Other equipment includes the Improved Entrenching Tool and its MOLLE cover (11).

A number of improvements to the MOLLE system resulted in the MOLLE II specification. A new type of M16 two-magazine pouch (8) made a brief appearance; it featured a quick-opening Velcro closure in place of the earlier combination of Velcro and snap. The MOLLE single-magazine pouch was discontinued. A late MOLLE development, the two-cell, four-magazine M16 pouch (9) was a transitional form, possessing features of the ILBE load-bearing system that was soon to follow. Other revisions included the improved patrol pack (see Plate B12); an integrated Fighting Load Carrier (FLC); a waist pack (essentially an improved butt pack); and a new 1-quart canteen/general-purpose pouch.

A typical MOLLE II rig for a Marine rifleman is shown at (10). Attached to the left side of the new FLC are two hand grenade pouches, affixed above two rifle magazine pouches of the earlier MOLLE pattern, and the new canteen/general purpose pouch. At center is the waist pack, and to its right the new IFAK and an additional M16 magazine pouch.

The new MARPAT utility uniform constituted a break from the joint-services combat uniforms worn by Marines in the 1980s and 1990s, its cut and material giving the Marine a distinctive appearance. In this photo, three sappers of the 6th Engineering Support Bn rehearse de-mining operations. (Cpl John E. Lawson Jr./USMC)

RIGHT Mounting numbers of burn casualties, resulting primarily from improvised explosive devices encountered in Iraq, led to a 2006 decision to re-equip Marines with flame-resistant clothing on missions "outside the wire." Nomex coveralls of the types used by air and vehicle crews filled the need until a new infantry uniform could be designed and issued. (Gunnery Sgt Mark Oliva/USMC)

combat shirt and trousers, complemented by a balaclava and gloves. The combat shirt is made of panels of different material composition to optimize breathability in areas covered by body armor (which itself confers flame protection), while offering flash protection to the exposed arms, shoulders and neck. In appearance, it resembles a knit jersey to which the collar and sleeves of an MCCUU have been grafted. Velcro attachment squares on the sleeve pockets for IR-reflective recognition tabs are a standard feature for the combat shirt. The combat trousers were designed to be of uniform flame resistance; they closely resemble the MCCUU trousers, with the exception of an additional "cigarette" pocket on each calf. The FROG combat ensemble was at first produced exclusively in Desert MARPAT to fill the urgent need in Iraq and for several years afterward. A Woodland MARPAT version became available in 2011. The Inclement Weather Combat Shirt (IWCS), a 2010 addition to FROG, provides a measure of wind and water resistance in colder and wetter climates; it is also of greater durability (a concern with the lighter-weight combat shirts) due to the reinforcement added to high-wear areas and the elimination of lightweight materials in its construction. FROG proved successful at limiting burn injuries, and the use of flame-resistant fabrics was eventually expanded to include the inner layers of cold weather clothing as well.

Extended Cold Weather Clothing System (ECWCS)

In the mid-1980s, the US Army and Marine Corps together developed a new cold weather clothing ensemble to replace an aging wardrobe having its origins in World War II. The new Extended Cold Weather Clothing System was a multilayered design using new synthetic materials. The ECWCS featured three insulating layers, a two-piece water-resistant Gore-Tex outer shell, and camouflage overwhites, comprising nearly two dozen articles of clothing in all. Most items were of new design, though a few existing items were adopted into the ensemble.

ECWCS insulating layers included polypropylene undergarments, a polyester Fiberpile middle layer, and quilted polyester jacket and trouser liners that constituted the outermost layer of insulation. These layers could be worn in varying combinations under the outer shell, or not at all, to suit environmental conditions. A variety of cold weather headgear, socks and handwear were also issued. The ECWCS shell consisted of a hooded parka and trousers constructed of Gore-Tex fabric to promote water repellency while allowing moisture vapor to escape, keeping the wearer relatively dry and warm. The existing snow camouflage overwhites were grafted into the ECWCS ensemble with only minor modifications; they included a full set of thin, quick-drying covers for parka, trousers, mittens, helmet and pack, offering no thermal protection but worn solely for concealment.

The bulky Extreme Cold Weather Boots issued with the ensemble are another older design. Also known as "vapor barrier" boots, they are constructed of insulating materials layered within a rubber skin to prevent evaporative cooling. Two types exist: Type I is rated to -20 degrees F and is made of black rubber, while Type II is rated for temperatures to -65 degrees F and is made in white rubber for camouflage in snow. They are known informally as "Mickey Mouse" (Type I) and "bunny" (Type II) boots. ECWCS handwear included Light Duty Work Gloves, Cold Weather Mitten Shells (Trigger Finger), and Extreme Cold Weather Mittens that could be worn over the trigger finger mittens when necessary. All types were provided with insulating liners.

The Marine Corps made minor modifications to the Gore-Tex parka and trouser shells in the 1990s, also introducing Polartec fleece insulating garments and improvements in gloves and mittens. The result was the USMC second-generation (Gen II) ECWCS – differing somewhat from a second

Flame-Resistant Organizational Gear, commonly known as FROG, became the first flame-resistant combat infantry uniform designed for the USMC. It is worn in this photo showing Marines of Battalion Landing Team 3/8 of the 26th MEU unloading gear upon arrival at Camp Lemonnier in Djibouti in the Horn of Africa. Note the distinctive appearance of the multi-material combat shirt, designed with a torso of plain "breathable" fabric for coolness under body armor. Some of these Marines also wear on their backs the hydration bladder of the ILBE equipment system. (Lance Cpl Tammy Hineline/USMC)

Marines attached to the 2nd MEU (SOC) wear Gen II fleeces during a mail call at an outpost in Hit, Iraq. Although designed as insulating liners – under, e.g., the ECWCS parka – rather than as jackets in their own right, fleeces have sometimes been worn as such when "inside the wire." (Sgt Richard D. Stephens/ USMC)

generation ECWCS produced by the Army. Although stocks of first-generation ECWCS continued to be issued until exhausted, the second-generation ECWCS was the predominant type in service at the beginning of the new millennium.

All-Purpose Environmental Clothing System (APECS)

Although ECWCS was a considerable improvement over its predecessor, neither the Marine Corps nor the Army was completely happy with even the Gen II improvements, and discussed sweeping revisions to the entire system to improve heat/moisture regulation, reduce bulk and drying time, and provide a more stealthy infrared signature. Another problem was that despite the updates introduced by the USMC and Army during the 1990s, ECWCS did not integrate well with newer combat equipment. Both services discussed options for an improved joint-service ECWCS, but ultimately each decided to pursue its own course. The Army retained the ECWCS designation, calling its improved system the Generation III ECWCS; the Marines chose to develop new cold weather clothing in two separate programs, termed the All-Purpose Environmental Clothing System (APECS), and the Mountain/Cold Weather Clothing System (MCWCS).

Released in 2004, APECS consists of a new parka and trouser outer shell to replace those of the Gen II ECWCS; it is best regarded as a refinement of the ECWCS shell rather than as an entirely new design. It too is made of Gore-Tex fabric and follows the same general construction as its predecessor, but is of much lighter weight, and features other modifications. These include, among others, the addition of side-opening breast pockets and a redesigned storm-resistant zipper closure. Most noticeable, however, is the replacement of the old Woodland camouflage pattern with Woodland MARPAT, which has also reduced its infrared signature. At the time of its introduction, APECS was worn with the insulating layers of the Gen II ECWCS system; replacement of these would have to wait a few years longer, for the advent of the Mountain/Cold Weather Clothing System.

Mountain/Cold Weather Clothing System (MCWCS)

A particular challenge faced in the design of cold weather clothing is that posed by human physiology: an active body produces far more heat than an inactive one, and any sweat produced during exercise will compound the chill experienced at rest. Although a system of layered undergarments will effectively handle a wide range of ambient environmental temperatures, it is less effective at responding to changes in body heat production – removing layers of body armor and load-carrying equipment on the march or in combat in order to change clothes is not a generally an option. When designing a new cold weather ensemble the USMC adopted an eminently practical solution: the ECWCS scheme of layered insulation within a weatherproof shell would be retained, but designers would include an additional highly-insulated layer that could be worn over everything else – to retain warmth while resting or engaged in less active tasks, and be removed before engaging in strenuous activity. Marines would now have a more practical way of quickly adjusting to changes in body heat production while retaining the environmental flexibility inherent in a layered system. The MCWCS combined these components with new head and handwear, plus a set of snow camouflage overgarments in the new Snow MARPAT pattern. The MCWCS is lightweight and designed to dry quickly; it is also compressible for a reduced packing volume – particularly important considering the added bulk of the outer insulated suit.

The three insulating layers are lightweight Next-to-Skin (also known as "silkweight") undergarments, midweight Grid Fleece, and Wind Pro Fleece. These layers replaced their second generation ECWCS equivalents. The shell is known as the Lightweight (LW) Exposure Suit, and consists of a Gore-Tex jacket and trousers similar in cut to APECS but of much lighter weight, and which can be stored very compactly. (The LW Exposure Suit overlaps somewhat in function with APECS, and is often worn in its place in snow-covered regions.) At the time of this writing, it has been produced only in Desert MARPAT, which is not always optimal for the environments in which it is used. The heavily-insulated MCWCS outer layer is officially called the Extreme Cold Weather Suit, but is known colloquially as the " happy suit". It comprises insulated parka, trousers and booties – the last are outerwear for use inside tents and sleeping bag, and not intended as a boot liner.

The MCWCS also includes a hard-face fleece ski cap or "beanie" that replaces the ECWCS cap. There are new Extreme Cold Weather Mittens and liners, and a new flame-resistant Light Duty Glove Insert (used in conjunction with the new mittens as well as the leather Light Duty Glove, which is not itself a part of MCWCS). The MCWCS snow camouflage overgarments consist of parka, trousers and pack cover in Snow MARPAT material. No helmet or mitten covers have yet been issued in the new Snow MARPAT, and the older solid-white covers continue in use. Unlike ECWCS, which is a full suite of cold weather gear, MCWCS is primarily a specification of a subset of new components. Consequently, other items of old and new cold weather

Col Robert Durkin, CO of the 25th Marines, speaks with staff at the Mountain Warfare Training Center (Bridgeport, CA) in 2009. They wear the APECS suit in Woodland MARPAT, and other recently-developed cold weather clothing. For additional warmth the Marine at center, equipped with a privately-purchased chest rig, wears the parka from his MCWCS "happy suit" – in plain Coyote Brown 498 color – over his APECS. (Cpl Tyler J. Hlavac/USMC)

An automatic rifleman of the 2/25 Marines simulates fire on an opposing force during *Cold Response* 2010, a multinational exercise hosted in Norway. *Cold Response*, formerly known as *Battle Griffin*, is conducted nearly every year. These Marines are wearing the Snow MARPAT camouflage ensemble, with the older solid white helmet covers. (Cpl Tyler J. Hlavac/USMC)

gear – such as scarves, gloves, vapor barrier boots and gaiters – are regularly worn with MCWCS components, as they are with the APECS shell. Regular updates of many of these items make any attempt at rigorous classification difficult at best.

The new ensemble was tested at the Mountain Warfare Training Center in Bridgeport, California, and components were initially supplied to field units during 2006–08. Most components of MCWCS are coyote brown in color, with the exception of the LW Exposure Suit and Wind Pro Fleece – produced in Desert MARPAT – and initial examples of flame-resistant undergarments, which began to appear in 2009–10 and were at first made in a light sand color. The new flame-resistant Next-to-Skin Underwear specifications now overlapped those of the FROG long-sleeved undershirt and served in both capacities. All of the new MCWCS undergarments eventually replaced their second-generation ECWCS predecessors, and could be worn with APECS as well as MCWCS.

Combat Desert Jacket (CDJ)

The Combat Desert Jacket is an item of cold weather gear specifically designed for use in arid regions. An innovative garment, this insulated lightweight jacket marries a number of dissimilar fabrics – each with a different function – into a single piece of apparel, much as does the FROG combat shirt. The upper and lower back panels of the jacket are made of a wind-resistant lightweight Gore-Tex fabric, whereas the middle back – where the CDJ might be in contact with a pack – is made of a more porous knitted material. The sleeves are made of a four-way elastic fabric, and the side torso panels are wind-resistant nylon fabric. Insulation is provided by a grid fleece lining. In keeping with its intended area of use, this garment is produced only in Desert MARPAT. Deliveries began late in 2007, following initial difficulties in producing a consistent color on the dissimilar fabrics used in its construction. The CDJ is an independent item and not part of a cold weather clothing ensemble like MCWCS.

Insignia and badges

Traditionally, Marines have worn few insignia in the field other than rank and the EGA, the latter appearing on the left breast pocket of the combat utility blouse and on the headgear. Whereas the EGA of older Woodland utility uniforms was applied in appliqué form by heat transfer, the EGA of MARPAT uniforms is embroidered. Pin-on rank devices are worn on the collar of field utility uniforms and on a tab provided on the center chest of cold-weather parkas. (Rank may also be worn on body armor in the same position). Name tapes and

Despite a traditional reluctance to wear identifying badges or insignia in combat, Marines are now more ornamented in the field than at any time in their recent history. In addition to name, rank and branch (sometimes on an embroidered nameplate), some Marines sport unit badges – as does this lance corporal of the 1/9 Marines patrolling in Ramadi, Iraq. (Lance Cpl Casey Jones/ USMC)

branch tapes similar to those worn by members of the other US Armed Services did not enter into regular use in the Marine Corps until the 1990s. These are sewn above the right and left breast pockets, respectively; an additional name tape is sewn above the right rear trouser pocket. More recently, name plates similar to those worn by military pilots have been adopted by Marine ground forces. US flag patches are sometimes worn by Marines as force identifiers on specific deployments and are not a part of the regular field uniform. Even colored adhesive tape is used: when applied to field clothing and equipment it can be a temporary way of marking a unit leader on exercise or in combat. Unit badges and other insignia are not authorized on field uniforms; however, landing and traffic support units are, by tradition, allowed red markings – a square on cap and helmet and red stripes sewn on the trouser leg – for the purpose of traffic management.

Members of a Landing Support Battalion (LSB) seen during an exercise in the late 1990s. The red patches worn on the helmet – along with a horizontal red stripe sewn to the trouser leg – identify these Marines as members of an LSB team, and are for recognition during amphibious operations. Here the IIFS load-carrying equipment is worn in conjunction with PASGT body armor. (CWO-2 Charles Grow/USMC)

During the wars in Iraq and Afghanistan, practice in the field has evolved – in part because of updates in regulations, but also because (as in all wars) regulations are not as rigidly enforced in combat zones as they are at home. Name tapes are often applied to helmets, packs and other items of gear; rank is also sometimes worn on the sleeve pocket of the utility uniform. Velcro-backed US flag patches, unit badges and other identifiers – not always authorized – are seen regularly in combat theaters.

PERSONAL PROTECTIVE EQUIPMENT

In the face of an increased frequency of conventional and unconventional battlefield threats in Iraq and Afghanistan, Personal Protective Equipment (PPE) assumed a particular significance in the Marine's kit. Just as recent combat experiences underscored the need for flame-resistant clothing, so they also prompted the development of improved types of body armor, and – despite the absence of a specific CBRN threat – CBRN protective equipment also remains important. Although the Marine infantryman entered the 21st century with a full complement of protective equipment, development of improved PPE in the following years was greatly accelerated from its peacetime levels, in order to enhance protection, reduce weight, and improve integration with other equipment.

This security checkpoint chief at the Fallujah Civil-Military Operations Center wears an Interceptor Outer Tactical Vest. Note the separation of the armored panels as he raises his arm, exposing his side. This shortcoming of the OTV design was corrected by the development of side armor panels, a stopgap measure that did not entirely satisfy Marines. (Cpl Mike Escobar/USMC)

Body armor

Nowhere are these rapid developments more evident than in the area of body armor: no fewer than a half-dozen armored vests were worn in the period 2000–2012 by regular forces, apart from the additional designs used by vehicle crew and special operations personnel. (By comparison, only three infantry armored vests saw widespread use during the preceding 50 years.)

The standard body armor of US forces throughout the 1990s was the **Personnel Armor System, Ground Troops (PASGT)** armored vest. Composed of multilayered Kevlar cloth, the PASGT vest effectively stopped shrapnel, but was not designed to stop high-velocity projectiles such as rifle bullets. Although this vest had many positive attributes for its class, and did lead to a significant reduction in fragmentation casualties in comparison with its predecessors, the military began to look into expanding the degree of protection to infantry to encompass defense against direct fire from small

---

D

MARINES, 2005–2007

1: Lance corporal, Combat Logistics Battalion 8; Iraq, April 2005

She is attached to the 3/8 Marines during a raid on Karmah. Though officially noncombatants, at this phase of the occupation female Marines from support units began to be fully embedded into infantry companies for missions that might involve the searching of civilian women. The US had instituted a policy that female service members would conduct these searches to avoid giving offense to the local population, since Islamic law forbids men from touching women other than their relatives. Despite an ostensibly noncombatant role, these Marines frequently took part in fighting alongside the men. This Marine wears desert MARPATs and standard infantry MOLLE gear on her OTV, and is armed with an M16A2 rifle.

2: Weapons platoon assaultman; USA, 2006

On a stateside firing range, this Marine carries the Mk 153 SMAW rocket launcher. This system, developed in the 1980s, is supplied with a variety of rocket types for use against different kinds of target. The assaultman wears the new Lightweight Helmet with his OTV.

3: 1st Lieutenant; Iraq, August 2007

As a matter of policy, Marines in Iraq engaged with the populace to promote goodwill and gather information on insurgent activities; this officer speaks with an Iraqi boy during a patrol outside Fallujah. Of note are his flame-resistant Nomex flight suit and gloves, issued in response to a 2006 mandate intended to reduce burn casualties from Improvised Explosive Devices (IEDs). Many of his equipment pouches are non-standard; it was not uncommon for individual Marines or entire units to purchase commercial supplements to their issued gear, often from the same contractors that manufactured the official equipment. USMC regulations provided some latitude in this matter, particularly in light of the wartime strain on supply. One of this officer's pouches holds an AN/PRC-148 handheld radio (**3a**). His M4 carbine – by now standard for junior officers – is equipped with the Rifle Combat Optic (RCO) and AN/PEQ-2A target designator, mounted left of the barrel.

1

2

3

3a

arms, termed "ballistic" threats. This level of protection had already been accorded to aviators and special operations forces; it only made sense to extend it to general ground personnel, given the available technology and affordable cost.

True bullet-proof infantry vests had been designed before by combining ceramic armor plates with ballistic fabric – most notably the Ground Troops Variable Body Armor of the late 1960s, and the Ranger Body Armor of the early 1990s – but none had been deemed suitable for general issue, chiefly because of excessive weight, inadequate area of coverage, and other factors. Work began in the mid 1990s on the new armored vest, which would be designed to protect against both low-velocity fragmentation threats and small-arms fire, yet be light enough for general issue to all armed services. The Army, meanwhile, developed in 1996 a stopgap ceramic plate carrier for the PASGT vest – the Interim Small Arms Protective Overvest – to provide contingency small-arms protection until a new vest could be fielded.

The new vest that emerged, **Interceptor Body Armor (IBA),** consists of an **Outer Tactical Vest (OTV)** containing soft armor panels conferring fragmentation and 9mm projectile resistance, and **Small Arms Protective Insert (SAPI)** ceramic armor plates. SAPI plates, when inserted into pockets on the front and back of the OTV, add high-velocity projectile protection to vital areas, being capable of stopping conventional 7.62mm NATO ball rifle rounds. Building on lessons learned in the past, designers made the OTV a completely modular system, permitting not only the option of removable internal armor panels, but also removable armor attachments to increase the area of coverage to the neck, groin and other parts of the body. Commanders were no longer forced to use the monolithic body armor designs of the past, but now had flexibility in choosing an optimal balance of protection and weight for specific missions. IBA accessory attachments contain soft armor panels providing shrapnel protection similar to those in the main body of the vest, and include a collar, a throat protector and a groin protector.

Two additional armor supplements for the OTV have been produced, but never enjoyed much success. The **Armor Protective Enhancement System (APES)** extended the area of shrapnel protection to the arm and upper leg, but hindered movement. Another set of attachments, **QuadGard,** provided full arm and leg coverage, but was extremely heavy and could lead to heatstroke in the hot climate of Iraq. When it was used, QuadGard was generally worn by Marines with stationary rather than very active roles, such as HMMWV cupola gunners; even so, movement inside a vehicle was still very much hampered by its bulk.

The Interceptor OTV weighs approximately 9lb including soft armor inserts and standard neck and groin attachments. This weight is only slightly less than the PASGT vest it replaced, yet the OTV has better soft armor, provides a greater area of coverage, and can be lightened if necessary by

The addition of side armor plates gave wearers of the OTV considerably more protection than they enjoyed previously. This combat engineer (his Side-SAPI carriers installed upside-down) removes mortar rounds from a weapons cache discovered in Al Anbar province of Iraq during Operation *Iron Fist* in February 2006. (Cpl Mark Sixbey/USMC)

removing accessory attachments. When the OTV is combined with SAPI plates the total weight is increased to 16lb, still less than previous bulletproof designs. Unlike earlier armor vests, the OTV was designed to integrate fully with load-carrying equipment, and even to act as its central component. Designed in conjunction with the Modular Lightweight Load-carrying Equipment (MOLLE) that made its debut around the same time, the OTV included a **Pouch Attachment Ladder System (PALS)** – a horizontal array of webbing to which pouches and other MOLLE-compatible equipment could be attached and repositioned at the wearer's discretion. The OTV shell has been produced in a number of camouflage colors, which is simpler than providing camouflage covers as was done for the PASGT vest. The OTV was first produced in Woodland camouflage for all services, and initial USMC deliveries were in this pattern; vests delivered on later USMC contracts have been in solid coyote brown.

Ceramic armor inserts, acting in concert with the soft armor panels of the Interceptor Body Armor system, saved the lives of many Marines in Iraq and Afghanistan. This scout from 3rd Light Armored Recon Bn holds the ESAPI plate that stopped a sniper's bullet. (Cpl Graham Paulsgrove/USMC)

Although front and rear protection is excellent, the Achilles' heel of the Interceptor lies in the loosely overlapping soft armor panels over the sides of the torso, which provide no ballistic protection; worse, being held together only by elastic straps, they will separate in certain postures, denying the wearer any lateral protection at all. In response to reports from Iraq of excessive casualties caused by small-arms fire and shrapnel wounds to this area, the **Side SAPI (S-SAPI)** plate was developed. A smaller version of the main SAPI plate, this slips into a carrier that attaches to the vest to protect the vulnerable lateral torso, and has proved highly successful in decreasing casualties. Improvements in armor plates also led to the **Enhanced SAPI (ESAPI)** and **Enhanced Side SAPI** plates, which provide protection against many types of armor-piercing rounds in addition to ball ammunition.

Combat experiences revealed other shortcomings in the OTV, and one complaint (shared by users of the earlier PASGT vest) was that it was too hot. To resolve this problem the Evaporative Cooling Vest (ECV) was developed, a moisture-wicking mesh garment for wear underneath the OTV. Another problem was that the added weight of side plates and other new attachments not in the original design specifications caused sagging, thus opening gaps in coverage, and increasing the fatigue of the wearer. In addition, the front Velcro closure of the OTV did not withstand explosive blasts as intended, sometimes being blown open. Both the Army and USMC felt that the piecemeal additions to the OTV had overtaxed the design and that the best solution lay in its replacement, which each service pursued independently.

Acting on an Urgent Universal Need Statement, the USMC developed the **Modular Tactical Vest (MTV)** in an accelerated development cycle that paralleled that of the Army's similar Improved Outer Tactical Vest. The MTV was rushed into production for general issue in 2007, intended as a short-term means of addressing the shortcomings of the OTV. It continued the design philosophy of a modular combination of carrier vest, soft armor panels and ceramic plates. The MTV features several improvements: a cummerbund to hold side armor more securely and keep the vest together in explosive blasts; a quick release to allow rapid emergency removal; improved load-carrying to lessen discomfort and fatigue; communications channels and a rifle bolster; a mesh liner for better cooling; and increased soft armor coverage to the torso and lower back. It has a similar basic set of modular soft armor attachments – collar, throat, groin and side. The throat armor is designed to fit more loosely, to allow the lower face to be tucked into it during indirect fire attacks for better protection.

Initial excitement among Marines eager to receive the new vest soon turned to disappointment when they discovered that its advantages were offset by its considerable weight: 30lb with full armor – much heavier than the OTV, and even heavier than earlier systems that had been rejected for general issue for that reason. The weight of a fully-loaded MTV, when combined with that of a typical Marine's other combat gear, greatly hindered mobility and accelerated fatigue. To many, the balance between protection and mobility had tipped too far to one side; in some circles the MTV even acquired the nickname "HESCO," after a type of earthworks employed in military fortifications. Sentiment was so strong that the initial procurement was placed on hold by the USMC Commandant, pending an investigation. Ultimately, the merits of the MTV design were judged sufficient to warrant its use in place of the OTV, though the latter would remain the official USMC body armor on record until the arrival of a longer-term replacement.

Although this decided shift toward protection at the expense of mobility was quite understandable in Iraq, where operations consisted of short counterinsurgency patrols in a flat landscape peppered with roadside bombs – an environment in which the MTV performed well – matters were quite different when Marine commitments shifted to Afghanistan, where rugged terrain, high altitude and frequent firefights favored lighter body armor. The

E   INFANTRY SMALL ARMS

The USMC arsenal expanded considerably during the first decade of the 21st century, as the Corps addressed the challenges of counterinsurgency operations while maintaining preparedness for conventional battles. A greater use of shotguns like the M1014 **(1)** was one result, as was the adoption of a common rail mount for attaching new targeting devices to all small arms (including the M1014). This rail system is shown to effect on the new M16A4/M203 Modular Weapon System **(2)**, here fitted with AN/PVQ-31 Rifle Combat Optic (RCO) and AN/PSQ-18 grenade launcher sight/laser target designator. The new 9mm M9A1 pistol **(3)** features a rail underneath the muzzle for mounting a weapon light, and other improvements over its predecessor M9. The M27 Infantry Automatic Rifle **(4)** is the successor to the M249 Squad Automatic Weapon. Like the M249, it uses the SU-258/PVQ Squad Day Optic, and can mount a variety of target designators including the AN/PEQ-16A.
The M32 Multi-Shot Grenade Launcher **(5)** adds considerable

firepower at the company level. The M136 **(6)** and improved M72 **(7)** series missile launchers have seen service in both Iraq and Afghanistan. The M84 stun grenade or "flash-bang" **(8)** and M67 fragmentation grenade **(9)** represent the diverse requirements of infantry missions. The M249 SAW **(10)**, here equipped with collapsible stock and M145 telescopic sight, formed the backbone of the infantry fire team until the introduction of the M127 IAR.
The OKC-3S Multi-Purpose Bayonet **(11)** replaced the M7 bayonet in 2003, but has not dislodged the venerable KA-BAR combat knife, which holds considerable symbolic significance for Marines. A number of accurized rifles have been developed for the newly-created category of Designated Marksman; one is the M14-derived M39 Enhanced Marksman Rifle **(12)**, which can be fitted with a number of day or night optics, including the AN/PVS-10 sniper scope shown. The M240 **(13)**, here mounting an SU-260P Machine gun Day Optic and A/N PEQ-16 target designator alongside the barrel, is the standard medium machine gun of the USMC

1

2

3

4

5

6

7

8

9

10

11

12

13

Marines of Combat Logistics Bn 4 are fitted with new Modular Tactical Vests in April 2007. The MTV provided greater fragmentation protection than the OTV, and better load-carrying properties, but was criticized as excessively cumbersome. (Sgt Ethan E. Rocke/USMC)

short-term solution chosen by the Corps was the creation of a lightweight complement to the MTV to be issued to Marines deploying to Afghanistan. The design that emerged in 2008, the **Scalable Plate Carrier (SPC)**, is just what its name implies: a carrier for ceramic armor plates. It uses the same set of front, back and side ceramic armor plates, but is radically scaled back in terms of soft armor coverage to an area little greater than that of the ceramic plates themselves. The SPC can use the MTV groin attachment, though has no provision for neck protection. Lower back protection is provided by a fold-down pad sewn into the back panel similar to that on the MTV. The SPC also uses a cummerbund in its design; though this lacks a quick-release feature, the cummerbunds are interchangeable between the MTV and SPC, and Marines often used their MTV cummerbund in both vests. To further simplify construction, the front and back soft armor panels are permanently integrated into the SPC, though the side panels and their carriers are removable. Weighing about 8lb less than the MTV, the SPC was seen as a great improvement in the combat conditions of Afghanistan.

After accumulating combat experience with both the MTV and SPC, further design limitations were identified, prompting the decision in 2009 to develop an improved version of each. The new armor included the **Improved Modular Tactical Vest (IMTV)** and **Plate Carrier (PC)**. The IMTV is about 2lb lighter than the MTV, and has redesigned shoulders for comfort and to lessen a particularly unpleasant shortcoming of the MTV: the potential for a rifle butt to slip during firing, hitting the shooter in the face. The IMTV also relocates the shoulder fasteners to the front for easier release in emergency. The cummerbund retains its quick-release capability and is simplified, with interchangeable right and left sides. PALS area coverage was increased as well.

The PC (known during development as the ISPC – Improved Scalable Plate Carrier) is a medium-weight successor to the SPC; it shares the common set of four ceramic plates with other designs, while offering soft armor coverage between that of the MTV and SPC. The side armor carriers were moved to the inside to prevent snagging and chafing (external carriers are unique to the SPC); shoulder release buckles were also moved to the front as with the IMTV. The IMTV cummerbund was adopted, giving cable quick-release capability to the PC. Field trials of the PC and IMTV were performed in 2010, but because of delays the vests did not begin to see general issue until late in 2011. At the time of writing, the PC is expected to become the primary body armor of the USMC, replacing the OTV – still the program on record – until the next generation of body armor is developed.

Experience with prodigious numbers of mines and improvised explosives in Iraq and Afghanistan led the USMC to consider the adoption of additional

The Scalable Plate Carrier was developed as a lightweight alternative to the MTV for use in the rugged terrain of Afghanistan, where mobility is at a premium. The trade-off between weight and protection can be appreciated by comparing the previous photo of the MTV with this shot, showing a security platoon commander directing a stranded vehicle recovery effort in the Nawa district of Helmand province. (Cpl Paul Zellner/ USMC)

body armor to protect the pelvic area from blasts underfoot. The groin armor of existing vests shielded the wearer only from lateral threats, and the USMC had no comparable equipment since retiring their 1950s-era lower torso armor. In 2011 an Urgent Statement of Need was issued for such protection, resulting in the interim adoption of the British Ministry of Defence **Pelvic Protection System (PPS)**, which comprises two components: a heavy silk Tier 1 PUGz Protective Undergarment (known informally as "ballistic boxers") to protect against low-impulse fragmentation injuries to the pelvic area; and the Tier 2 Protective Over Garment (POG), a close-fitting ballistic armor cup – the latter worn over clothing, and resembling a codpiece. The USMC has supplemented its initial procurement of British-manufactured PPS with domestically-produced examples and is considering a new Tier 3 garment with broader coverage.

Helmets

The Marine Corps continued to use the 1980s-vintage PASGT helmet in forward infantry units during the earlier stages of the wars in Iraq and Afghanistan. The PASGT helmet, or "Kevlar," was a fragmentation helmet

designed to stop shrapnel but not small-arms fire. In an effort to develop a stronger and lighter replacement, the USMC introduced the Lightweight Helmet (LWH) in 2004. The LWH was developed in tandem with the Army's own PASGT replacement, the Advanced Combat Helmet (ACH). Both helmets are made from advanced, lightweight materials. Unlike the ACH, which sacrifices some coverage at the sides and back in return for improved integration with other equipment and additional savings in weight, the LWH retains the basic shape and area of protection of the PASGT helmet but still weighs a few ounces less. It features improved shrapnel protection and is capable of stopping a 9mm bullet. An improved four-point retention harness is used with the new helmet, offering greater stability than the two-point chin strap of the PASGT. A reversible Woodland/Desert MARPAT cover was introduced for the LWH, though older camouflage helmet covers for the PASGT are also compatible.

Marines received a helmet armor upgrade in March 2007, with the

A Marine corporal keeps watch in Husaybah, Iraq, during Operation *Steel Curtain* in November 2005. Husaybah had been the scene of intense fighting for the Marines the previous year, and resistance to the new offensive proved equally determined. This Marine wears the new Lightweight Helmet; typically, his utilities and load-carrying equipment are in different color patterns. (Sgt Jerad W. Alexander/USMC)

Side-by-side comparison of the USMC Plate Carrier (left) and Improved Modular Tactical Vest (right), in a Quantico demonstration room display. Both have a cummerbund feature, and are in coyote brown color. The PC and IMTV replace, respectively, the SPC and MTV. Also shown is an early example of the Enhanced Combat Helmet (ECH), which is intended to complement, rather than replace, the Lightweight Helmet in the USMC inventory. (Author's photo)

addition of the Nape Protection Pad (NPP) to extend fragmentation protection below the rim of the helmet – a clever way to increase the area of shrapnel protection without hindering head mobility. The NPP can be worn with any infantry helmet in the USMC inventory; in most cases, commanders have made its use optional for their Marines.

Two additional helmets have seen service with the USMC in more recent years, but adoption of the first was unplanned. The LWH program had been plagued for years by chronic manufacturing problems, creating a shortage which became acute in 2011; this prompted a contingency order of the Army's Advanced Combat Helmet for distribution throughout the Corps. The USMC expects to finally receive adequate quantities of the LWH late in 2012, at which time the ACH will be retired from service. An additional helmet design, developed in conjunction with the Army, was requested in a 2009 Urgent Statement of Need for Marines deployed to Afghanistan. Known as the Enhanced Combat Helmet (ECH), the new helmet is not unlike the ACH in general appearance and weight, differing primarily in its greater ballistic protection. The ECH is not intended as a replacement for the LWH, but for issue to Marines in overseas contingency operations. Following a number of developmental delays, the ECH is expected to become available in late 2012 as the mission to Afghanistan draws to a close.

Joint protection

Although soft polymer foam knee and elbow inserts have been developed for the MCCUU field uniform, hard plastic external pads are preferred, and a number of models of the latter have been worn by Marines in recent years. Knee pads have proven particularly useful during combat in urban and rocky terrain. (Elbow pads are less practical for general use, and are worn infrequently.) Early in the war in Iraq, Marines typically wore commercial models purchased by unit commanders or individuals; it was not until 2004 that the USMC adopted an official pattern for general issue.

Eye protection

The human eye is the body's most vulnerable sensory organ: it can be harmed by dust, the sun's ultraviolet rays, and, on the battlefield, by laser light and shrapnel. In the 1980s the US military began development of eyewear with laser and impact protection to improve on the basic protection from debris and light offered by the standard issue Sun/Wind/Dust Goggles (SWDG). Work led to the Ballistic/Laser Protective Spectacles (BLPS), issued with a set of interchangeable impact-resistant polycarbonate lenses, two of which were designed to block specific wavelengths common to military lasers. Similar laser-filtering ballistic inserts were also developed for the SWDG. A second spectacle design fielded in 1998, the Special Protective Eyewear, Cylindrical System (SPECS), featured comparable

Marines of Combat Logistics Bn 11 conduct a casualty evacuation drill in October 2011. They wear a combination of the Army-designed Advanced Combat Helmet and Marine MTV body armor – opposites in design philosophy *vis-à-vis* the trade-off between protection and weight. The Marine at left carries his sidearm in a FILBE holster. (Cpl Tommy Huynh/USMC)

protection. These spectacles and goggles were in service with Marines in the first years of the 21st century.

New specifications designed to integrate eyewear with night vision devices and other equipment led to new goggles and spectacles, under the rubric Military Eye Protection Systems (MEPS). MEPS consists of the Profile NVG goggle and the ICE 2.4 Eyeshield spectacles, both with impact-resistant lenses and manufactured by Eye Safety Systems. The Profile NVG goggle was issued to Marines in limited numbers beginning in 2002, but was not fully fielded for another two years. Laser-protective inserts were not initially provided but have since become available. Individual Marines have also worn a number of commercial protective eyewear designs, not all of which provided adequate ballistic protection. In response, the USMC compiled a list of approved commercial alternatives meeting military specifications; during the wars in Iraq and Afghanistan it was not uncommon for a mix of eyewear to be worn within a single platoon.

Hearing protection

Noise-induced hearing loss is a common but often overlooked injury among combat veterans, becoming more evident as they age. Increasing awareness of this problem led the Marine Corps in 2000 to institute the Marine Corps Hearing Conservation Program, and, in 2012, to institute mandatory annual hearing tests for all Marines. New materials and technologies have been employed in the past decade to prevent hearing loss by one of two principles: passive protection, in which the materials and shape of the ear plugs attenuate sound, and active protection, in which electronic filters detect harmful noise and send an inverted-phase duplicate directly into the ear, effectively cancelling it.

The USMC entered the 21st century with the standard military ear plugs issued in previous decades, which offered broad attenuation of all sounds to about 25 dB. Although helpful on the firing range and for artillery crews, they were less useful for infantry in combat, as they blocked ambient sounds as well as loud noises – so critical sounds such as footfalls, orders or communications from squadmates could be missed.

A Marine stands security during an August 2004 raid against Shia strongman Muqtada al-Sadr in An Najaf, Iraq. Knee pads, often purchased by unit commanders or individuals during the early occupation, were particularly appreciated by Marines involved in street fighting. (Cpl Daniel J. Fosco/USMC)

In 2005 an improved form of passive hearing protection was introduced. Called Ballistic Hearing Protection, or Combat Arms Earplugs, the new earplugs have two modes of attenuation, depending on how they are inserted: one end – color-coded green – is useful for attenuating steady-state noise, while the other – colored yellow – selectively filters out loud noises but allows lower-volume sounds to pass through. A second type of new device, the QuietPro Integrated Intra-Squad Radio Hearing Protection Headset (IISR-HPH), acquired in 2007, provides active protection. Connecting directly to radio communications equipment, it actively attenuates harmful acoustic peaks with an inverted-phase signal broadcast directly into the ear, while allowing softer sounds to pass without dampening. The IISR-HPH also accommodates voice-activated transmission and programmable control.

Chemical, Biological, Radiological and Nuclear protective equipment

In an effort to simplify defense logistics, the various CBRN protective suits of the US armed services were replaced in 1997 with a common standard: the Joint Service Lightweight Integrated Suit Technology (JSLIST) protective overgarment. The JSLIST is a lightweight, hooded two-piece suit having little bulk, and is easily carried. Protection for up to 24 hours of exposure is given by a chemically-absorbent liner containing a matrix of embedded activated carbon spheres within a water-resistant outer shell. The JSLIST is nearly identical to its USMC predecessor, the Saratoga suit, differing only in minor aspects of tailoring. It is the Saratoga, in fact, that most Marines wore during the 2003 invasion of Iraq – their single large-scale use of CBRN equipment in battle since the 1991 Gulf War. Both the Saratoga and JSLIST are issued with rubber gloves, boots and gas mask.

The health protection officer of the US Marine Corps Forces, Pacific, is fitted with an M40 gas mask during annual chemical weapons training at "K-Bay," the Marine base at Kaneohe Bay, Hawaii. The 1980s-era M40 was in use until 2009, when it began to be replaced with the more advanced M50. (Lance Cpl Ronald W. Stauffer/USMC)

The USMC adopted the M40 series chemical protective mask in the 1990s. The M40 includes voicemitters for communication, a drinking tube interfacing with a port in the canteen drinking cap, and a single filter that can be mounted on either side to suit right- or left-handed riflemen. The mask is designed for continuous use in contaminated environments for up to 12 hours. The M40 was replaced by the M50 in late 2009. Its chief advantages are an endurance of up to 24 hours, matching that of the JSLIST suit, and its lighter weight. It uses two smaller filters rather than the single filter of the M40, and positions them lower to avoid interference when firing a weapon. Both the M40 and M50 are issued with a web carrier, worn at the left thigh for ready use.

Marines of the 24th MEU check their M50 Joint Service General Purpose Masks for fit during training at Camp Lejeune, North Carolina, in 2011. They wear the Saratoga CBRN suit; the JSLIST, its 1997 replacement, differs only in minor details of tailoring. CBRN suits have a limited shelf life, so stock is rotated and older suits are placed in service before new suits. During training older, pre-used suits are worn so as to conserve new sealed equipment for contingencies. (Lance Cpl Michael Petersheim/ USMC)

Several types of CBRN detection equipment are also issued. M9 detector tape reveals the presence of liquid chemical agents, and is worn around the ankle, wrist or arm of the protective suit. Although the tape detects the presence of such agents, it cannot identify them; the M256A1 chemical agent detector kit can be used to identify a number of chemical hazards. Recently developed detection equipment includes the ID badge-size Chemical/ Biological Individual Sampler (CBIS); the handheld Joint Chemical Agent Detector (JCAD); the larger man-portable or vehicle-mounted Automatic Chemical Agent Detector Alarm (ACADA); and the Joint Biological Point Detection System (JBPDS).

LOAD-CARRYING EQUIPMENT

In the mid 1980s the Marine Corps, in conjunction with the US Army, explored ways to improve the distribution of the foot soldier's basic equipment. The All-purpose Lightweight Carrying Equipment (ALICE) suspender and waist belt system in use at the time concentrated the load at the waist belt, as had previous systems. This arrangement, while adequate, provided limited space for equipment and presented problems in ergonomics. A new load-bearing vest was considered to be the best solution, since this could make use of the entire torso to distribute equipment more evenly. (Several special-purpose load-bearing vests had been designed by the US military in the past – most famously, the ill-conceived Assault Jacket worn during the June 1944 Normandy landings – but none had yet been adopted for general issue.)

Integrated Individual Fighting System (IIFS)

The new vest, designed at the US Army's research and development center in Natick, Massachusetts, moved rifle ammunition and grenades from their former location in pouches mounted on the waist belt to a series of fixed, integral pockets positioned across the front of the vest, effectively

redistributing the load and freeing space on the waist belt. This ITLBV was at the heart of a new set of equipment, the **Integrated Individual Fighting System (IIFS)**. In addition to the load-bearing vest, made in separate versions for riflemen and grenadiers, the IIFS also included a new pack system and sleeping system. The former combined a main pack with an integral frame that gave much-improved support over the simple ALICE frame. A small patrol pack was provided for missions of short duration, and this could simply be "piggybacked" on top of the main pack for full marching order.

Rather than a true replacement for ALICE, IIFS was a supplement. The vest did replace the ALICE suspenders and (nominally) the magazine pouches, but the other components of ALICE were retained – even the ALICE magazine pouches served on occasion to carry additional ammunition or other gear. The IIFS was intended for primary issue to infantry, so many support units continued to use ALICE in its original form, and it also persisted to some degree in Marine infantry battalions.

Modular Lightweight Load-carrying Equipment (MOLLE)

Although the essential features of a tactical vest and dual-pack system were appreciated, criticism was directed at the inflexibility of the new IIFS vest. Its pockets were sewn in fixed positions, preventing customization for varying types of missions; the vest also trapped body heat, making it uncomfortably hot. Work on a new system of load-carrying equipment was carried out jointly by the Army and Marine Corps in the late 1990s, building on the positive features of IIFS. Called Modular Lightweight Load-carrying Equipment (MOLLE), the new system introduced the Pouch Attachment Ladder System. PALS allowed the interchangeable attachment of MOLLE pouches at a variety of positions on the vest, to tailor their configuration

A fire team refill magazines during an August 2000 exercise at the Marine Corps Air-Ground Combat Center at Twentynine Palms, California. The newly-issued MOLLE gear carried by this group is the early pattern, which suffered from unnecessary complexity and a problematic rucksack connector. Note the supplemental 1-quart canteens carried in conjunction with the new 3-liter hydration bladder. Early models of the new hydration system were not equipped with a gasmask-compatible drinking tube, making it necessary to retain the old canteen for the sake of its NBC drinking port. (Sgt Donald R. Storms Jr/USMC)

A Marine of the 26th MEU returns to the USS *Bataan* in January 2002 following missions to Kandahar at the opening of operations in Afghanistan. He wears early-pattern MOLLE equipment over Interceptor body armor. Covering (and not quite fitting) his OTV is a camouflage cover designed for the earlier PASGT vest. (Chief Photographer's Mate Johnny Bivera/USN)

according to mission or personal preference. In the PALS attachment system, vertical straps on the back of a pouch would be woven through complementary horizontal straps on a vest or other equipment for a secure fit. A new Load-Bearing Vest (LBV) was developed. It was designed to be worn in concert with either of two types of waist belts that were provided: a molded waist belt for use with the MOLLE pack system, and a utility belt for lighter load orders. To minimize heat retention, the corset-like back panels of the ITLBV vest were left out of the LBV design, which was supported at the back by two simple vertical straps. PALS straps covered the front and sides of the vest and the belts, so pouches could be attached almost anywhere. As mentioned above, consideration was given from the start to the integration of body armor into the load-carrying equipment. The OTV, developed concurrently with MOLLE, featured the same PALS as the MOLLE vest, permitting the wearer two options for carrying his equipment: on the vest, worn over body armor when required; or mounted directly on the OTV, doing away with the LBV entirely. This feature would later prove immensely practical during the long years in Iraq and Afghanistan.

Several pouches were designed for the MOLLE system: 30-round single and double magazine pouches for the M16, single and double pouches for 40mm HE grenades, a double pouch for 40mm pyrotechnic grenades, a 9mm single magazine pocket, a fragmentation grenade pocket, a 200-round pouch for the M249 Squad Automatic Weapon (SAW), and a 100-round/utility pouch that served a variety of purposes – this was most often used to carry linked rounds for the M249, rifle magazines, or 40mm grenades. A KA-BAR combat knife adapter was provided to Marines; ALICE adapters extended the compatibility of MOLLE to older equipment such as the old 1-quart canteen and ALICE carrier, which were both retained in MOLLE. These were supplemented by a new 100oz (3-liter) hydration bladder worn on the back. The hydration bladder and its drinking tube were much more convenient than a canteen, but because the new hydration system was incompatible with the standard gas mask drinking system, the 1-quart canteen with its CBRN-compatible port was still an essential item of equipment. Specific sets of pouches were issued in kit form for different occupational specialties: rifleman, SAW gunner, grenadier and corpsman (medic) each received a unique combination of MOLLE pouches. Corpsmen, in fact, were issued a unique medical pack and pouches for carrying their equipment.

The MOLLE pack system retained the dual patrol and main pack system of IIFS, but increased the degree of modularity further. Rather than a large IIFS-style pack to contain most items of kit, the MOLLE system featured a smaller main pack with a detachable sleep-system carrier underneath; a butt pack, virtually identical to the earlier ALICE training field pack, was also included. Two supplemental sustainment pouches could be attached to the sides of either the main pack or patrol pack if additional cargo capacity was required. The pack system featured PALS, so MOLLE pouches could be attached wherever needed. The frame of the main pack was designed to connect to a molded waist belt associated with the LBV by an innovative socket-and-probe mechanism. (Alternately, the molded waist belt could be permanently attached to the pack frame by those opting to use the utility belt with their LBV.) A removable SINCGARS radio pouch was included with the main pack, as was a bandolier capable of carrying six M16 magazines.

MOLLE II and "USMC MOLLE"

Although initial deliveries of MOLLE to the Marine Corps early in 1999 were well received, several shortcomings were identified, prompting a number of revisions. The major problem was a tendency of the main pack frame to bounce free of its socket on the molded waist belt during vigorous activity or if mounted improperly; this was both an inconvenience and an opportunity for lower back injury. The socket-and-probe system was done away with, and the molded waist belt was permanently attached to a newly-designed frame. The system of dual waist belts was now redundant, and features of the utility belt and LBV were combined to create the Fighting Load Carrier (FLC) vest (which was itself refined in subsequent years with a number of small modifications). Other changes included elimination of the single-magazine M16 pouch, simplification of the double-magazine pouch, addition of a new 1-quart canteen carrier (this also serving as a general utility pouch), and replacement of the butt pack with a slimmer waist pack. The revised MOLLE system was officially termed MOLLE II, though both are often referred to simply as "MOLLE."

Early examples of MOLLE equipment delivered to the Marine Corps were made in the old Woodland camouflage pattern, but following a 2003 specification equipment destined for the USMC began to be produced in coyote brown. Other differences between Army and Marine Corps MOLLE began to appear as new MOLLE II equipment was developed by each service semi-autonomously. In addition to the KA-BAR adapter designed for the Marine Corps under the original MOLLE specification, a carrier for the USMC Improved Entrenching Tool was developed, as was a two-pocket M16 magazine pouch with a four-magazine capacity. Both services designed a "dump" pouch for collecting spent magazines, though the Marine version was intended to be worn as a part of an individual's load-carrying equipment and the Army pouch was vehicle-mounted. Both services also designed a replacement for the old joint services Individual First Aid Kit (IFAK) to their own specifications. The new USMC IFAK adds a hemostatic agent and tourniquet to the basic medical supplies of the old kit. The contents are organized into two packets: one containing general first aid and water purification items; the other a trauma kit, designed to stop arterial bleeding. The new IFAK is carried in a larger, MOLLE-compatible carrier.

Improved Load-Bearing Equipment (ILBE)

Although MOLLE marked a considerable advance over previous designs and was an excellent system overall, the Marine Corps was still not entirely happy with the pack system. This sentiment, combined with a growing divergence of view between the USMC and Army over the future direction of MOLLE development, led to a parting of ways. The Army continued its refinements under the MOLLE II designation, while the USMC pursued its own improvements under the rubric of Improved Load-Bearing Equipment. The ILBE specification included a new two-part pack system, hydration system, load-carrying vest, and set of ten equipment pouches. The ILBE

A Navy corpsman sets off on skis during a cold-weather medicine course at the USMC Mountain Warfare Training Center in 2009. He carries a standard ILBE main pack and piggybacked assault pack (the special Corpsman Assault Pack would more likely be issued for a combat deployment), to which are fastened an IFAK and a sleeping mat. For this training maneuver he carries a replica carbine molded in solid blue plastic. (Cpl Nicole A. LaVine/ USMC)

system of pouches is in most regards a variation of MOLLE rather than an entirely new system. It retains the modular PALS attachment system at the heart of MOLLE, and compatibility with most MOLLE equipment, but differs in its accommodation of USMC-specific kit and in smaller details. (The development of ILBE parallels a second set of USMC load-carrying equipment, Full-Spectrum Battle Equipment (FSBE). The two systems share many features, but because FSBE is intended for special units – Force Recon, Fleet Anti-Terrorism Security Teams, and MEU (SOC) helicopter assault companies – rather than for general infantry use, it will not be discussed here.)

The ILBE pack system is another matter: it arose from a desire for a pack with greater simplicity, comfort and durability than the original MOLLE system, with special features adapted to USMC requirements. Rather than initiating a lengthy design process the Corps adopted a commercial backpack, the Arc'teryx Bora 95, and added a few modifications. The new pack system features a main pack and assault pack (similar in function to the MOLLE patrol pack) that can be piggybacked like the MOLLE equivalents. The ILBE main pack combines the functions of the old MOLLE main pack and sleep-system carrier. It features a contoured, ergonomic frame for better fit, and load-lifter straps that allow the wearer to adjust the load toward upper or lower back to reduce fatigue on long marches. This pack system is produced in a standard infantry version (S-ILBE) and a larger reconnaissance version (R-ILBE). Sustainment pouches can be attached to any ILBE pack, but in practice are issued only with the R-ILBE. In addition, a special Corpsman Assault Pack (CAP-ILBE) is issued to medical personnel in place of the standard assault pack. Several other components were introduced: Waterproofing Bag Inserts (WBI) and the Marine Corps Stuff Sack (MACS Sack) to keep cargo dry, and a redesigned radio pouch. The MOLLE 100oz/3-liter hydration system was adopted as a component of ILBE and issued with the new pack system; later, a new WXP Hydration System of the same capacity was introduced, along with an inline Individual Water Purification System (IWPS). The ILBE pack systems were fielded in early 2004.

F **BODY ARMOR & IMPROVED LOAD-BEARING EQUIPMENT**

The Scalable Plate Carrier (1) and the Modular Tactical Vest (2) represent opposites in design philosophy. Both have accommodation for two side armor plates in addition to front and back plates, but they vary dramatically in soft-armor coverage and overall weight. The MTV is shown with one each of its Enhanced SAPI and Enhanced Side SAPI plates exposed.

ILBE is the Marine Corps successor to MOLLE, and comprises a new pouch set and pack system. ILBE pouches share the PALS attachment system and full compatibility with MOLLE, being a refinement rather than a replacement, and are used in concert with the MOLLE FLC vest. Ten types of ILBE pouches are used in combinations depending upon position within the squad and platoon. The combination shown at (3) is typical for a unit leader equipped with the M203 and wearing the MTV. (Top row, left to right:) three pouches for 40mm HE rounds, and one or two (one shown) for M67 hand grenades;

(bottom, left to right:) an IFAK; a multi-grenade pouch – here with a smoke grenade; pouch for a "pop-up" star parachute flare; three M16 single/double pouches; M16 magazine speed reload pouch; and a "dump" pouch to hold spent magazines. Other ILBE pouches include a 200-round SAW/utility pouch with removable internal partition (4); a 9mm pistol magazine pouch (5) – here with the cover flap stowed for quick access to the magazine – see Plate G4 for closed flap; and a pouch holding ten 12-gauge shotgun shells (6). The MOLLE "Storm" hydration system was re-issued with ILBE, as was a new WXP 3-liter system, shown with an inline Individual Water Purification system installed (7); the uninstalled IWPS is shown at (7a).

The infantry ILBE pack system includes a standard main pack, the S-ILBE (8), issued with an internal radio pouch (9), and an assault pack (10). Both come with waterproof liners and the waterproof Marine Corps Stuff Sack. A more capacious version of this pack system was produced for Recon troops, but is beyond the scope of this book.

1

2

3

7

7a

4

5

6

8

9

10

Men of the 1/2 Marines undergo an equipment inspection. They carry a full combat load in the ILBE pouches festooning their MTVs and in the packs at their feet. These Marines wear WXP Hydration Systems on their backs. (LCpl Scott Schmidt/ USMC)

Work also began on a new load-carrying vest, designated the Assault Load Carrier (ALC), and a new set of pouches. Although the ALC was cancelled in favor of keeping the MOLLE FLC, a new group of ten ILBE pouches was developed. The new pouches afford similar functionality to the older MOLLE gear, but include new types that are better-suited to USMC requirements. The ILBE pouch group consists of an M16 single/double magazine pouch; an M16 (single magazine) speed reload pouch (so-called because of its ease of magazine extraction – it is designed to be the pouch of choice in an emergency); a 9mm 15-round magazine pouch; single 40mm grenade pouch; pop-up flare pouch; M67 grenade pouch; 12-gauge shotgun shell pouch; multi-grenade pouch (designed to hold smoke, incendiary, star cluster and flash-bang grenades); 200-round Squad Automatic Weapon/ utility pouch (with removable internal partition to allow storage of rifle magazines or grenades); and dump pouch (somewhat different than the MOLLE version) for spent magazine collection. Some pouches, such as the SAW/utility pouch and dump pouch, are provided with PALS webbing on their front face to allow the fixing of additional pouches. In addition to the hydration system and FLC, other specific MOLLE items are intended for use with the ILBE system (and all MOLLE items are compatible). These include the MOLLE 1-quart canteen/utility pouch and improved entrenching tool carrier. Unlike the hydration system, which has a dual MOLLE/ILBE identity, the FLC and other items retain their MOLLE designation.

Family of Improved Load-Bearing Equipment (FILBE)

The ILBE main pack, despite its excellent quantities, was not designed to be worn over body armor, and did not integrate optimally with the existing OTV or new types of body armor that became available. In addition, a quick removal feature for pouches was sought to aid combat vehicle crewmen in the tight confines of their stations and dismounted troops needing to transfer pouches between MTV and SPC between missions (Marines in Afghanistan received both vests), a cumbersome process at best. These and other considerations prompted a new round of equipment R&D, resulting in the Family of Improved Load-Bearing Equipment specification. FILBE replaces the ILBE pack system with a new set of packs and hydration carriers called the USMC Pack System. Other FILBE components expand the ILBE group of pouches, adding several new items of load-carrying equipment to the existing set.

In many ways, the new USMC Pack represents a convergence with Army refinements of the MOLLE main pack. It features greater modularity than the ILBE main pack, including multiple sustainment pouches and hydration pouches, and is more MOLLE-like in appearance – boxy, rather than tall and narrow. It integrates better with body armor, and induces less fatigue

than the ILBE. A larger assault pack, new 100oz hydration system and new assault pouch are also a part of the USMC Pack System. The new pack system was tested in 2011 and will be fielded in 2012.

Other FILBE components include a pistol holster replacing the M12, and the USMC chest rig. The USMC Holster is essentially a SERPA II commercial holster, a favorite private-purchase item. Available in versions for the M9 and M45 pistols, the USMC Holster is a hard-shell, quick-release design. It allows a much faster draw than the M12, which is an important factor in combat, but criticism has been leveled at the design because of its potential for jamming and accidental discharge. The USMC Holster has a modular mounting system allowing its wear at the hip, on a thigh rig, or on any equipment with a PALS ladder.

The new USMC Chest Rig combines several types of load-carrying pockets into a single torso-spanning unit that can quickly be detached and transferred between body armor vests. It is issued with adapters for all current vests, and can also be worn with a separate webbing harness. The chest rig is also useful for vehicle crew who need to remove pouches quickly when entering or leaving the confines of their vehicle. It contains six single-magazine rifle pouches, two utility pockets, and three administrative pockets on the reverse side. A PALS ladder across the front allows Marines to attach additional equipment. This rig was tested in Afghanistan in late 2010, and began to be issued in quantity in 2011. The final component of the FILBE specification is the Corpsman Assault System, which would combine an updated Corpsman Assault Pack with several other items of load-carrying equipment designed for medical use. The CAS is under consideration for procurement in 2012–13, though at the time of this writing the CAS program is still at an exploratory stage.

A squad leader of the 1/3 Marines spreads goodwill during a security patrol with Afghan National Army soldiers in the Garmsir district in May 2011. He is equipped with the new Chest Rig over his SPC. Unlike MOLLE and ILBE pouches, this can be quickly transferred between the MTV and SPC to give tactical flexibility to Marines stationed in Afghanistan, who are issued both these types of body armor. The Chest Rig was also designed with combat vehicle crews in mind, providing them with a load-bearing system that can be taken off and put on again quickly when entering and leaving the confines of an armored vehicle. (Cpl Colby W. Brown/USMC)

Other load-carrying equipment

Although most load-carrying equipment fits into one of the classifications discussed above – or at least is closely affiliated with it, as the new Individual

First Aid Kit is with ILBE/FILBE – many exceptions exist. Some items such as map cases predate the modern load-carrying equipment categories; other items are closely associated with a particular type of equipment rather than any load-carrying system. These include disposable bandoliers in which ammunition and other ordnance are distributed and carried; spare barrel carriers for machine guns; pouches for binoculars and weapon sights; weapon cases such as the Gunslinger (a backpack issued to snipers to conceal their rifles), and many more. In addition, many Marines – particularly those deployed to combat areas – carry commercially-produced load-carrying equipment that they or their commander have purchased privately.

BIVOUAC & SPECIAL-PURPOSE ITEMS

This sergeant of the 2nd Light Armored Recon Bn has turned his OTV into a portable office. Many Marines quickly discovered that the PALS webbing system is ideal for holding small necessities, and their OTVs blossomed with marker pens, scissors and multi-tools. (Lance Cpl John A. Faria/ USMC)

The USMC issues a water-resistant field tarpaulin and quilted poncho liner in Woodland MARPAT that have replaced the older Woodland camouflage poncho and liner. The field tarp is a traditional and versatile item of equipment that can be used as a tent section, ground cover, a wrap for shelter or concealment, and almost anything else a Marine can think of.

The 3-Season Sleep System (3S) is the current sleeping bag set. It expands the endurable temperature range by -15° F, and weighs a pound less than the Modular Sleep System (MSS) used previously. The 3S is often used in conjunction with a foam polymer sleeping mat, as much for insulation as for comfort. A self-inflating mat is now also available. The compact, collapsible Enhanced Bed Net System (EBNS), an improvement of the Improved Bed Netting System (IBNS), is an individual portable shelter that provides rain and insect barriers for sleeping Marines. Stoves for heating rations or melting snow/ice for drinking water are also issued. The improved entrenching tool, described above, is a replacement for the steel tri-folding shovel and features a light-weight polymer handle.

A number of special-purpose kits and equipment are available to Marines. A Mechanical Breacher's Kit (MBK) offers Marines an alternative to the use of explosives or special shotgun rounds in the forced entry of buildings. It

contains a bolt cutter, sledge hammer, Halligan bar and other tools to quickly breach locked doors and windows. Marines deploying to cold weather regions are issued the Marine Corps Cold Weather Infantry Kit (MCCWIK), which includes a cook set, cargo sled, snow saw and hatchet, ski climbing skins, and other basic equipment for a four-man fire-support team in cold environments. Military cross-country skis and snowshoes are also issued. Three types of snowshoes have been used in the past decade, including an older racquet-like magnesium snowshoe, a "bear paw"-shaped composite design with tubular frame, and the current Modular Steel Traction Snowshoe (MSTS), a lightweight polymer snowshoe featuring detachable floatation tails, pivoting bindings and steel cleats. The current-issue skis have been in use for 30 years, but are no longer produced and are heavy in comparison with more modern equipment. At the time of writing, the Marine Corps is searching for a suitable replacement. A Marine Assault Climber's Kit (MACK) is provided for use in mountainous regions and enables an infantry company to perform vertical ascents up to 300ft in height. The MACK is provided in both Alpine and Ice modules (for areas with and without snow, respectively) and is assembled from off-the-shelf commercial climbing equipment.

Marines are issued a number of instruments and sensors, depending on their role in the infantry battalion and current mission. These may include a lensatic compass, shock-measuring helmet sensor, GPS device, the CBRN detection equipment discussed above, and a number of other devices. One recent innovation is the Handheld Weather Station (HHWS), issued to unit leaders in mountainous areas and to scout-sniper teams to monitor meteorological conditions.

Observation and illumination

The M22 7x50 binocular is the standard US military field optic. Two models exist: the Steiner M22 that has been produced for decades, and a model by Fujinon that entered service more recently. The M24 is a compact 7x28 binocular. The USMC also uses the 8x42 Tactical Infantry Binocular, a lightweight design by Leupold. The M49 spotting telescope is used for observation. Many of these optics may be used in conjunction with an anti-reflection device, commonly known as a "killFLASH"; this consists of a short, honeycombed tube attaching to the front of the binoculars or telescope to block lens reflections that could reveal an observer's position.

In the late 20th century night vision equipment began to feature more heavily in US tactical doctrine, and improvements in passive detection technology and miniaturization have encouraged this trend. These devices fall into two categories: image intensifiers, which amplify existing light; and thermal sights, which detect infrared emissions – particularly those of personnel and warm engines. In recent years the USMC has fielded the AN/PVS-7 series Generation 3 image intensified night vision monocle, which may be handheld or helmet-mounted. This model is being replaced by the AN/PVS-14 Monocular Night Vision Device (MNVD), a smaller, lighter-weight night vision monocle. The AN/PVS-14 can also be used as a weapon sight.

A particular drawback to monocular devices is the loss of depth perception. The AN/PVS-21 Low-Profile Night Vision Goggles (LP-NVG) are true binoculars, and can integrate data from sensors and other inputs directly into the visual display. Several handheld thermal imagers have also been fielded, including the AN/PAS-22 Long Range Thermal Imager (LRTI)

– a binocular, handheld replacement for the older SOPHIE system – the AN/PAS-28 Medium Range Thermal Bi-ocular (MRTB), and the AN/PAS-30 Mini Thermal Imager (MTI).

In the realm of portable illumination, the MX-991/U crookneck flashlight has long been the US military standard. Newer designs have been added in recent years, including the Streamlight Sidewinder Handheld Flashlight (HHF), a handheld/helmet-mounted flashlight. The Sidewinder is lighter and more compact than its predecessor, and operates with LEDs rather than an incandescent bulb. Whereas the MX-991/U was capable of only visible light (white, or colored by means of plastic filters), the Sidewinder can produce infrared light for use with night vision optics. It also provides visible light in white, blue (for following blood trails), and red (for reading maps). The Sidewinder was acquired in late 2009. Also fielded is the Ultra-High-Intensity Illumination System (UHIMIS), a long-range visible and IR source of illumination.

Communication equipment

The handheld portable radios carried by infantry platoons are the forward components of a broader combat network, yet in the past these devices had little compatibility with other parts of the net. Units in combat were restricted to line-of-sight, short-range ground communications using radios that were not always reliable. Rapid advances in electronic and digital technologies in the 1990s made possible portable radio sets with greater capabilities within a much more sophisticated combat net. Planners designed a force-wide, networked information technology system to seamlessly integrate encrypted voice and data communications with software tools to improve the situational awareness of commanders, and the coordination of combined arms – a process that continues under the Joint Tactical Radio System (JTRS) program.

At the beginning of the 21st century Marine commanders relied on a number of interim handheld radios, termed the Handheld Radios Family of Systems, to overcome limitations of the AN/PRC-126 Integrated Intra-Squad Radio (IISR), a product of 1970s technology. In response to a 1999 Urgent

A chief warrant officer demonstrates battery replacement during a 2005 presentation on the use of AN/PVS-7 night vision goggles. (Lance Cpl Cristin K. Bartter/USMC)

A team from the 6th Civil Affairs Group pose for the camera after a meeting with community leaders in Fallujah, Iraq, in October 2005. This team is equipped with the AN/PRC-343(V)1 Personal Role Radio (PRR) adopted from the British Army, a radio that proved invaluable during the fighting in Iraq. The USMC purchased some 10,000 PRRs to overcome shortcomings of squad communications equipment, keeping them as an interim measure until the advent of newer US models. (Lance Cpl Josh Cox/USMC)

Statement of Need one such expedient, the British Army's H4855 Personal Role Radio, was adopted by the USMC as the AN/PRC-343(V)1 IISR. Despite an incompatibility with other radios, this UHF radio offered much-improved tactical communications to infantry squads and platoons, and served for several years until the arrival of new handheld models. A second interim IISR to be introduced was the AN/PRC-153, a lightweight secure radio also operating in the UHF range.

Other handheld radios fall into the category of Tactical Handheld Radio (THHR), a more capable cousin of the IISR. Experience in Afghanistan and Iraq underlined the importance of linking squad communications with the combat network, and a THHR is designed for full interoperability with other radios on the net, to allow forward teams to link securely with other MAGTF elements. Special adapters also allow these radios to connect directly to vehicular systems for improved range. The first THHR, the AN/PRC-148 – a.k.a. Multiband Inter/Intra-Team Radio (MBITR) – was in production for the US Army by 2000 and was introduced within the Marine Corps in limited numbers, but gradually found broader use as an interim radio. A second interim THHR with similar features is the AN/PRC-152. The THHR and IISR can be used in conjunction with the QuietPro active noise attenuation device described earlier. IISR and THHR are both slated for replacement when the Joint Tactical Radio System becomes fully implemented.

The function of team command and control is typically carried by both THHR and by larger portable radios. The PRC-119 Single Channel Ground and Airborne Radio System (SINCGARS) family of combat net VHF radios emerged in the 1990s. The SINCGARS is capable of carrying long-range encrypted voice and data transmissions by line-of-sight and (through UHF transceiver) by satellite uplink. The SINCGARS is produced in both manpack and vehicle-mounted versions. An improved combat net radio, the AN/PRC-117 Multiband Radio – a 2008 JTRS initiative offering considerably broader bandwidth, processing speed and other capabilities including streaming video – has replaced many of the SINCGARS radios in service. Other new manpack radios include the AN/PRC-150 High-Frequency Radio, a replacement for the legacy AN/PRC-104. One particularly important use for the HFR is to relay communications from reconnaissance and air/naval gunfire liaison teams to operational headquarters.

INFANTRY WEAPONS

Small arms developed in the years following 2000 have been in large part based on older designs, some of which have existed half a century or even longer. The greatest changes in recent years are not in the weapons themselves, but in target acquisition devices. Recent years have seen the development of a variety of day and night sights, laser and visible-light target illuminators, and (for missiles) improved guidance systems. Another key advance has been the introduction of a universal mounting system, creating modular weapons with places to quickly attach these new devices, and to reconfigure them as the mission dictates.

Bayonets and fighting knives

Although the bayonet is seldom used in modern combat, most fighting forces around the world keep it on the books. To replace the M7 bayonet, which had been in service since the Vietnam War, in 2003 the USMC fielded the Multi-Purpose Bayonet (MPB), a new design combining features of a bayonet and fighting knife. The MPB, also known as the OKC-3S, is a heavier, larger bayonet than the M7, and began to be delivered to Marines shortly before the invasion of Iraq. In contrast to bayonets, utility knives are often needed on a daily basis. The MPB is also a functional fighting and utility knife; nevertheless, the Mark 2 combat knife – better known as the KA-BAR – that has come to symbolize Marine *ésprit de corps* is still issued, just as it has been since its introduction during World War II.

Pistols, rifles, carbines and shotguns

The standard sidearm of the USMC since the 1980s has been the 9mm Beretta M9 pistol, updated in 2006 with a Mil-Std-1913 universal rail mount (described below) and other improvements to produce the M9A1. Formerly issued to weapons crews, Marine officers, staff NCOs and attached Navy personnel, it was replaced in most billets with the M4 carbine following a June 2006 change in policy. The M45 Close Quarter Battle Pistol (CQBP) is an updated version of the .45cal M1911, issued to Special Operations Command (MARSOC) personnel.

The M16A2 service rifle in use during the invasions of Iraq and Afghanistan had changed little from the M16A1 that Marines carried 30 years earlier. Although updates to the fire control system, sights, barrel and ammunition were made in the 1980s, the core design was very much the same. In absence of a clear replacement, the USMC and Army modernized the aging M16A2 in 1999 to improve target acquisition in what was known as the Modular Weapon System (MWS) program. The MWS centered on the development of a common rail-mounting system for all small arms, the Mil-Std-1913 rail accessory interface. Generally referred to as the Rail Adapter System (RAS), it was the means by which a variety of sights, night vision devices, target illuminators, weapons lights and other accessories could be attached, removed or repositioned to reflect changing mission requirements.

Because the mounting system was universal – intended for adoption on all small-arms types – common accessories could be developed for use on a variety of weapons. The M16A4 MWS rifle that emerged had a new upper receiver and handguard with integral RAS. The USMC began fielding the M16A4 in 2003, completing its transition from the M16A2 in 2007. Another change was the replacement of the traditional two-point sling by modern three-point slings, which allow small arms to be carried more comfortably and brought to bear more quickly. One-point slings are also sometimes used. In 2012, a modified two-point sling improving on the features of the three-point sling was chosen as the new standard service sling for rifles, carbines, and the M27 Infantry Automatic Rifle.

The USMC has traditionally favored exclusive use of the full-length battle rifle for infantry, eschewing the carbine. This view has changed in light of recent actions – particularly in close urban environments – to which shorter, lighter weapons are better suited. The M4 carbine Modular Weapon System was adopted in 2003 to fill this role, and, in 2006, it replaced many of the M9 pistols in service. Like the M16A4 MWS, the M4 features both single-shot and burst fire, and a standard Mil-Std-1913 rail. The M4A1 Close Quarter Battle Weapon (CQBW), a full-automatic variant of the standard M4, is also in the USMC inventory, but is generally reserved for sniper teams, reconnaissance, special response teams and MARSOC.

Shotguns have seen considerable use in the USMC in recent years, particularly as secondary weapons. The most common types in the inventory are the Mossberg 500 series (500A1 and A2) and Remington 870 12-gauge pump-action shotguns, and the semiautomatic Benelli M1014 12-gauge Joint Service Combat Shotgun (JSCS). Infantry teams are issued shotguns at their commander's discretion for specific roles or actions; they have figured prominently in the street fighting in Iraq and Afghanistan.

A 6th Marines sergeant pauses after a meal alongside his squad's weapons at a location outside Fallujah in early 2006. Note the profusion of combat optics, weapon lights and grip attachments that can be mounted to the Mil-Std-1913 rails now shared by all Marine small arms. Also of some interest is the fact that on close inspection the sergeant can be seen to wear a 1990s-vintage nighttime desert parka. Although rendered obsolete by the improved IR characteristics of modern desert clothing, the darker tones of this parka can still be advantageous in certain conditions, particularly for scout snipers and designated marksmen. (Gunnery Sgt Mark Oliva/USMC)

Sniper and Designated Marksman rifles

A number of new rifle types have been fielded in recent years, in large part to supply the newly-created category of "designated marksman," but also to accommodate the evolving needs of scout snipers. Most are new designs belonging to the M16 family, or are derived from the existing M14 rifles held in arsenal storage since the 1970s. Marine Corps scout snipers typically use scoped rifles in two calibers, 7.62mm NATO and .50-caliber. The latter is particularly useful at long range and in cases where penetrative power is needed, such as attacks on light vehicles. The mainstay of scout sniper armament is the M40 sniper rifle, based on the Remington Model 700 and first put into service during the Vietnam War – an excellent weapon, effective up to 900 metres. It has been updated several times: the A3 model was developed in 2001, replacing the A1, and

additional improvements, including suppressor capability, resulted in the M40A5 in 2009.

The bolt-action M40 does have limitations, including a low rate of fire, heavy weight and distinctive sound signature. The Mk 11 Mod 1, a 7.62mm derivative of the basic M16 design, was acquired in limited numbers in 2006 as an expedient to address these shortcomings. This rifle offered accuracy at medium ranges combined with a higher rate of fire, and was used to complement rather than replace the M40. The Mk 11 was replaced in 2011 by an improved version, the M110 Semi-Automatic Sniper System (SASS). The M110 is also issued alongside the M40; scout snipers have the option of carrying either or both together, depending upon the nature of the mission.

The Barrett .50-cal semiautomatic M82A3 Special Application Scoped Rifle (SASR) and its lighter-weight 2007 replacement, the Barrett M107 SASR, are employed to disable light vehicles and against fortifications and similar targets at ranges of up to 1,800 metres. Explosive Ordnance Disposal (EOD) personnel also use the Barrett to destroy explosive devices from a safe distance. The USMC does not at present have a long-range anti-personnel sniper rifle to complement this primarily anti-matériel weapon, but is evaluating options for a new weapon that it is calling the Precision Sniper Rifle (PSR).

The "designated marksman" is a relatively new phenomenon in the US military. Unlike scout sniper teams, which are battalion-level assets that typically engage targets at long distance from a fixed position, the designated marksman (also known as a squad advanced marksman) is an organic part of the rifle squad and participates directly in small-unit actions. Designated marksmen engage targets at intermediate ranges in support of their squad or platoon, and a number of M14- and M16-based weapons chambered in 5.56mm and 7.62mm have been developed for this role. Lighter weapons include the Squad Advanced Marksman Rifle (SAM-R), an accurized, scoped M16 service rifle fielded in 2001; and the Mk 12 Mod 1 Special Purpose Rifle (SPR) – also called the Mk 12 Designated Marksman Rifle – which replaced it in 2009. Heavier weapons based on the 7.62mm M14 service rifle include the Designated Marksman Rifle (DMR) – which should not be confused with the Mk 12 DMR described above – and the M39 Enhanced Marksman Rifle (EMR). The DMR, a contemporary of the SAM-R, is an accurized, scoped M14 with a custom stock. Its replacement, the M39 EMR, is also built from an M14, but differs from the DMR most noticeably in its alloy, railed chassis with collapsing stock. The M110 is replacing the M39 as the USMC seeks to eliminate redundancies in its arsenal. These 7.62mm

ABOVE LEFT Lioness Program volunteers adjust the sights of their M16A2 rifles during live-fire training at Camp Korean Village, Iraq, in July 2006. The Lioness Program in Iraq, like the Female Engagement Teams in Afghanistan, trained female Marines to conduct searches of Muslim women and children so as to avoid offending local cultural sensitivities. Since these duties had to be performed while fully embedded with infantry companies, they put an extra premium on weapons range practice for female Marines. (Staff Sgt Raymie G. Cruz/USMC)

ABOVE A Marine scout sniper fires his Barrett M82A3 .50cal rifle at the Combined Arms Training Center at Camp Fuji, Japan, in 2006. Note the worn desert paint finish that speaks of prior deployments to the Middle East or Southwest Asia. (Lance Cpl Kevin M. Knallay/USMC)

weapons are also used by EOD, security and anti-terrorist personnel.

Squad automatic weapons and machine guns

The M249 Squad Automatic Weapon has been the standard squad support weapon for the past quarter-century. The M249 is a belt-fed light machine gun sharing a common 5.56mm NATO rifle cartridge with the M16 and M4. Ammunition drums are available in 100- and 200-round capacities, and these, plus its compact size, make the M249 a highly portable weapon, although it is twice the weight of rifles of similar caliber. The SAW has undergone several changes over the years; most significantly, it has recently been given the universal Rail Adapter System and can mount RAS-equipped accessories. The M249 is an aging weapon, however, and increasing problems with reliability, as well as a desire for a lighter weapon, have led the Marine Corps to seek a replacement.

A machine-gun team from Battalion Landing Team 1/2 of the 24th MEU mans an ad hoc vehicle checkpoint outside Sheik Mazar, Iraq, in January 2005. This team is armed with a profusion of weapons, including the M240G medium machine gun, M16A4 rifle, M136 missile launcher and M9 service pistol. (Lance Cpl Caleb J. Smith/USMC)

A lighter alternative, the M27 Infantry Automatic Rifle (IAR), was introduced in 2010. Derived from the M16 rifle, the M27 is a magazine-fed weapon comparable to a rifle in weight and accuracy – an improvement on the M249 in both respects. Because its 30-round magazine and fixed barrel restrict its capacity for sustained fire, its adoption will force considerable changes in infantry squad tactics, even though a larger, 50-round magazine

---

H   COLD WEATHER CLOTHING & EQUIPMENT

1: Designated marksman; Afghanistan, 2011

This Marine on patrol in the mountains wears the All-Purpose Environmental Clothing System (APECS) underneath his Scalable Plate Carrier and pelvic Protective Overgarment (POG); initial examples of the latter were acquired from the British Ministry of Defence, so it appears in British Multi-Terrain Pattern camouflage. The DM has the new Rugged All-Terrain boots; the US Army's Advanced Combat Helmet, issued in 2011 to address a shortage of standard USMC Lightweight Helmets; and FILBE chest rig, with pouches on the front for a Mk 67 frag grenade and a multipurpose utility tool. He is armed with a silenced Mk 12 Mod 1 SPR, one of many new rifles developed for designated marksmen; here it mounts the standard TS-30A2 telescopic sight and an AN/PEQ-16A target designator. The rifle magazines he has chosen are a commercial model of polymer construction.

2: Marine reservist, 2/25 Marines; Exercise *Battle Griffin*, Norway, 2005

This reservist pulls a cargo sled along a march route during a multinational winter warfare exercise held in Norway – note the blank-firing adapter fitted to the muzzle of his M16. Underneath his overwhites he wears the second-generation ECWCS suit and OTV body armor; he is also outfitted with MOLLE gear. His snowshoes are made from lightweight metal tubing and PVC plastic, with cleats for improved traction. The cargo sled is a component of the Marine Corps Cold Weather Infantry Kit, designed around the needs of a four-strong fire team.

3: Fire team leader, 2/25 Marines; Norway, 2005

The fire team leader has elected to wear his body armor and load-bearing vest under his overwhites for improved camouflage. Visible secured to his pack is a sleeping mat – very important when bivouacking on frozen ground.

4: Automatic rifleman, 2/25 Marines; Exercise *Cold Response*, Norway, 2010

He now wears the Snow MARPAT suit over APECS cold-weather clothing, and has new flame-resistant glove liners. The Snow MARPAT set includes a pack cover (not shown), but no helmet cover: the old solid white covers are still used. He carries an ILBE pack with sleeping map lashed to the side. Despite the considerable demands upon the USMC supply chain at this time, this reserve Marine is outfitted largely with new equipment, in part because of the active role Marine Forces Reserve plays in the Corps' global commitments. Although this reservist's OTV would not be worn in a combat theater at this late date, the remainder of his ILBE kit would be typical of any full-time infantry unit serving in Afghanistan. He wears Expedition Crocodile mountaineering gaiters with his Type 2 "bunny" boots, and lightweight Modular Steel Traction Snowshoes; the latter, with their modular plastic body construction (only the cleats are steel) and pivoting bindings, mark a departure from previous designs. He is armed with an M249 SAW fitted with an M16 blank-firing adapter – a common, though not ideal choice. The new heat-resistant M240/M249 Spare Barrel Bag (5) replaced the older vinyl-impregnated carrier, which was susceptible to damage when hot barrels were exchanged.

1

5

2

3

4

Marines of Battalion Landing Team 1/9 of the 24th MEU provide security during a training exercise at Camp Lemonnier, Djibouti, in March 2009. Note the RCO sights and AN/PEQ-15 target designators fixed to their weapons. (Sgt Alex C. Sauceda/USMC)

is in development. Infantry companies will still retain a number of M249s for discretionary use in a sustained suppressive fire role. Fielding of the IAR is expected to be complete in 2012.

Medium and heavy machine guns include, respectively, the M240 and M2. Originating as the Belgian MAG58, the M240 is a 7.62mm belt-fed design dating to the1950s. It has been fielded in two principal infantry models by the USMC: the M240B, a ground-employed infantry model, and M240G, a universal model capable of being configured for infantry, ground vehicle or aerial roles. Like other small arms, the M240 was updated with RAS mounts. The Browning M2 .50-cal machine gun, born of a November 1918 prototype, is still in use by the USMC. Although it is supplied with a tripod, it is usually mounted on vehicles.

Small-arms sights and target illuminators

A large number of sighting aids have been fielded in conjunction with the RAS to improve target acquisition in all conditions, day or night (see panel). These include: simple reflex sights for close-quarters combat; day telescopic sights; image intensifiers and thermal imagers for night vision; laser target illuminators, and weapon-mounted flashlights. Several reflex and telescopic sights have been evaluated by the Marine Corps over the past decade. Unlike the Army, which in the late 1990s adopted the M68 Close Combat Optic reflex sight for general issue, the Corps made a more limited use of reflex sights, ultimately assigning them to reconnaissance and special operations personnel who are most likely to see combat at close range, where these sights are most effective.

Several models have been used, including the Trijicon RX01 and M68; as of this writing, the Eotech Holographic Diffraction Sight (HDS) is the principal reflex sight in use. The USMC selected a telescopic sight for general issue to ground forces, reflecting its traditional emphasis on marksmanship. The standard M16 rifle scope is the 4x32 AN/PVQ-31A Rifle Combat Optic (RCO) – a member of the Trijicon Advanced Combat Optical Gunsight (ACOG) family of telescopic sights. The M4 carbine uses the AN/PVQ-31B, which has a reticle calibrated to the ballistic properties of its shorter barrel. Day scopes have also been developed for automatic support weapons. The Elcan M145 has been used with the M249, and was replaced in 2008 with the SU-258/PVQ Squad Day Optic (SDO). The SDO is also used on the M27 IAR. The SU-260P Machine gun Day Optic (MDO) is used with the M240. "KillFLASH" anti-reflection attachments are available for most sights.

Throughout the 1990s the Corps relied on the AN/PVS-4 night vision scope for much of its nighttime target acquisition capability. By 2011, however, a profusion of night vision devices of much greater sensitivity – both image intensifiers and thermal imagers – had been fielded for individual and crew-served weapons (see panel). Considerable use has also been made of target illuminators for small arms. These devices include weapon-mounted flashlights – the Visible Light Illuminator (VLI) and VLI Replacement (VLIR) made by Surefire – and laser target designators, such as the AN/PEQ-2 series Target Pointer/Illuminator/Aiming Light (TPIAL) that entered service at the turn of the millennium. The TPIAL can be used with a variety of RAS-equipped weapons, and is typically mounted on rifles, carbines, squad automatic weapons and machine guns. It uses an infrared laser pointer that functions with night vision goggles, making the source impossible to detect without night vision equipment. Smaller, more rugged models have since replaced the TPIAL, and have been complemented by specialized types designed for exclusive use with the M203 grenade launcher and M9A1 pistol.

A number of day and night scopes have been adopted for specific use by snipers and designated marksmen. The current day scope for the Barrett .50-cal and most 7.62mm rifles is the Scout Sniper Day Scope (SSDS), which replaces the Leupold M series and Unertl scopes formerly used. The TS-30 A2 day scope is used for all 5.56mm weapons, while the A1 variant is used with the 7.62mm DMR. Night vision sniper scopes include the AN/PVS-10 and AN/PVS-27 Scout Sniper Medium Range Night Sight (SSMRNS).

Common small-arms sights, image enhancement devices and target illuminators
Reflex sights: RX01, M68, HDS
Day telescopic sights:
Rifle/carbine: AN/PVQ-31 series; SSDS and TS-30 series (snipers only)
Automatic Rifle: M145, SU-258/PVQ
Medium MG: SU-260P
Sniper/marksman: SSDS, TS-30A1 and A2
Night vision devices:
Image intensifiers: AN/PVS-4, -10, -14, -17 series, -24A, -27
Thermal imagers: AN/PAS-13D series, AN/PAS -27
Laser target illuminators: AN/PAQ-4, AN/PEQ-2 series, -6A, -15, -16, -16A, AN/PSQ-18A

Grenades and grenade launchers

Explosive grenades in the USMC inventory include the M67 fragmentation and Mk 3A2 offensive concussion grenade. The latter is especially useful at close quarters, where fragmentation grenades might pose a risk to the thrower. Smoke grenades include the AN-M8 HC white smoke, used for signaling and screening, and the M18 colored smoke grenade used for signaling; the latter comes in a variety of colors, and is usually carried by squad and platoon leaders. Incendiary grenades include the M15 white phosphorus (also used for signaling) and AN-M14 TH3 grenades. The M84 stun grenade, better known as the "flash-bang," produces a blinding flash of light accompanied by a clap of extremely loud noise to temporarily incapacitate enemy personnel. Several CS (tear gas) grenades are also available to USMC forces.

The M203 40mm grenade launcher is a breech-loading, single-shot design mounted underneath the barrel of an M16 rifle or M4 carbine. Ammunition includes HE, dual-purpose HE, canister, star flares (parachute and cluster), and CS gas rounds. The M203 is issued with a simple leaf sight for quick shots in combat; a more accurate quadrant sight is also provided, but takes longer to aim, so is not useful in all combat environments. The M79 grenade launcher – the predecessor of the M203 – is still in service in a limited role. In 2010, the USMC fielded a stand-alone grenade launcher of South African design: the M32 series Multi-Shot Grenade Launcher (MSGL). The M32 is

A Marine of Combat Logistics Bn 6 trains with the M32A1 Multi-Shot Grenade Launcher at Ft Bragg, North Carolina, in April 2011. With a six-round rotary magazine, the M32 MSGL is a stand-alone semi-automatic grenade launcher of South African design, recently adopted by the Corps to supplement its M203 series launchers. (Staff Sgt Richard McCumber/USMC)

a semi-automatic launcher fed by a 6-shot rotary magazine, equipped with a RAS like other small arms. The older, belt-fed Mk 19 Automatic Grenade Launcher is still widely used by the USMC, and provides fully automatic fire for devastating impact. It can be tripod-mounted, but because of its bulk (73lb plus ammunition and tripod) it is usually emplaced on a vehicle mount. It fires a longer 40x53mm grenade cartridge in contrast to the 40x46mm ammunition used by the other grenade launchers.

Anti-personnel explosives

The M18A1 Apers directional anti-personnel weapon or Claymore, a design dating from the 1960s, is still issued. This is a shrapnel mine that can be detonated on command or by means of a tripwire. It is issued in kit form, in a disposable bandolier. Other, more generalized explosives are used by USMC combat engineers, but are beyond the scope of this book.

Rocket launchers

The USMC has at its disposal a number of shoulder-fired missile systems for infantry use. Unguided rockets include the improved M72 Light Anti-Armor Weapon (LAW), the M136 (AT4), and the Mk 153 Shoulder-launched Multipurpose Assault Weapon (SMAW).

A fire team leader from 3/4 Marines breaks through a mud-brick wall during a search of buildings in Now Zad, Afghanistan, in December 2009. Slung on his back is an M72 rocket launcher, useful for demolishing structures requiring more force than a sharp, well-aimed kick can deliver. (Sgt Jerad W. Alexander/USMC)

The improved M72 and M136 are short-range systems. These single-shot, disposable rockets do not require a specialist operator, but can be carried by ordinary rifle squad members in addition to a personal weapon. The 1960s-vintage M72 has received updates to both its launching tube and rocket ammunition. It now has a much greater range and is provided with any of several types of warheads, transforming it into a multipurpose system no longer limited to an anti-armor role. It has proven useful against bunkers and other targets in Iraq and Afghanistan, where its light weight and low cost in comparison with other systems stand to its advantage. The M136 was fielded in the 1980s to replace older versions of the M72 in an anti-armor role, as the original M72 was not sufficiently powerful to penetrate the armor of the newest Soviet battle tanks. The M136 has a much larger warhead than any model of the M72 (original or improved) and is now multipurpose, having a number of different projectile types. It is also larger, heavier, and – in the absence of large armor formations in current conflicts – has been less useful in recent years than the rocket launcher it was intended to replace.

The Mk 153 SMAW is a longer-range multipurpose system. Like the M72 and M136, its rockets are unguided, but the SMAW differs in having a reloadable launcher and is operated by a dedicated two-member team. The

Affording a clear view of Desert MARPAT utilities, this 7th Marines mortar team sets up an M224 60mm tube during a training exercise in Queensland, Australia. The M224 has been the standard company-level mortar of the USMC for several decades. Like its larger cousin the 81mm M252, it was lightened and improved in a 2011 modernization program. Incidentally, note the right-hand man's green utility belt, which identifies his martial arts ranking. (Lance Cpl Jerome E. Reed/USMC)

SMAW has a unique feature among US rocket launchers: an integral spotting rifle. The approved method of use is to fire spotting rounds at the target first to ensure a follow-on hit with the rocket, but this does expose the gunner for an extended length of time. Fielding of an improved SMAW II with a laser rangefinder in place of the spotting rifle will eliminate this vulnerability, and is anticipated in 2012. Other improvements of the SMAW II include reduced weight, and a new rocket that can be fired from within an enclosed space – the backblast of other rounds makes them suitable for outdoor use only.

Shoulder-launched guided missiles include the FGM-148 Javelin and its short-range cousin, the FGM-172 Predator Short-Range Assault Weapon (SRAW). The Javelin is a heat-seeking anti-armor rocket with greater range than unguided rockets, and replaces the wire-guided M-47 Dragon. The missile features a tandem warhead to defeat reactive armor; it can be fired in either a direct line-of-sight mode, or in an indirect parabolic arc to strike tanks in their thin top armor. It can also be used against helicopters and fortified bunkers. The Predator fills a niche similar to that of the M136. Like the Javelin, the Predator is capable of direct and parabolic modes of fire, but divides these modes between two classes of missile ammunition. In response

to changing priorities in Iraq, in 2005 the USMC converted its parabolic Predator missile rounds to the direct fire model for urban assault. This version is called the Short-Range Assault Weapon-Multiple Purpose Variant (FGM-172 SRAW-MPV).

The USMC retains one wire-guided anti-tank missile system for infantry: the TOW 2 Advanced Anti-tank Weapon System – Heavy (AAWS-H), an updated version of the 1960s-era TOW system. This heavy, long-range system is mounted on a HMMWV or on a tripod. Recent updates include the introduction of the Saber M41 Improved Target Acquisition System (ITAS) and refurbishment of existing stocks of TOW 2B missiles.

Anti-air defense is provided by the shoulder-launched FIM-92 Stinger heat-seeking surface-to-air missile (SAM).

Mortars

Infantry units are armed with 60mm and 81mm mortars. Currently the M224 60mm light mortar (company level) and M252 81mm medium, extended-range (battalion level) models are in use. Development of improved fire control and lighter weight construction was implemented in 2001 for improved use in urban operations, resulting in the M224A1 and M252A1 in 2011.

Non-lethal weapons

The increasing counterinsurgency and policing role performed by Marine infantry units alongside security forces in Iraq and Afghanistan prompted

Exhausted Marines practice the time-honored tradition of seizing any opportune moment for some expedient sack time. These members of the 11th MEU are back aboard the amphibious assault ship USS *Bonhomme Richard* after completing a noncombatant evacuation training exercise in 2009. (Gunnery Sgt Scott Dunn/ USMC) broader issue of existing non-lethal weapons to combat units. A Non-Lethal Weapon Capability Set (NLWCS), formerly issued only to anti-terrorist and force protection units, began to be issued to Marine rifle companies as well. An accelerated program of development and standardization of new NLW types under the Joint Non-Lethal Weapons Program (JNLWP) has also been set in place. NLW comprise a growing number of weapons including non-lethal munitions, incapacitating sprays, lights and lasers (stun and CS grenades, described above, rank among these.)

FUTURE DEVELOPMENTS

What do the coming years hold with regard to development and acquisitions of individual combat equipment? With a decade of counterinsurgency operations in the Middle East and Southwest Asia winding down – and wartime funding along with them – the USMC is reducing its force to a peacetime size, and making budget cuts as it assesses its future global priorities.

Although an exceptional number of developmental programs have concluded (or are being concluded at the time of this writing), new programs are always in progress, even if only at an exploratory stage. Building on recent experience with a pastiche of mutually impinging equipment architectures, the Marine Corps is continuing its emphasis on integrating all aspects of an infantryman's equipment to ensure optimum performance. Of particular importance at present are the ongoing development of a single new modular body armor model to replace the current "bifurcated" system; and a helmet electronics system that integrates visual display, sensors and communications to improve situational awareness on the battlefield. New infantry weapons, targeting aids and radio equipment are also in the works.

Although it may not always be possible to anticipate the precise form future infantry combat equipment will take, what is certain is that the traditional – and primary – role of the Marine Corps as an amphibious expeditionary force will grow in importance as the Pacific Rim assumes a greater strategic significance to the United States, and that the design of future infantry combat equipment will reflect this return of the USMC to its roots.

GLOSSARY OF ACRONYMS USED IN THIS TEXT

3S: 3-Season Sleep System

ACADA: Automatic Chemical Agent Detector Alarm

ACOG: Advanced Combat Optical Gunsight

ALC: ILBE Assault Load Carrier project

ALICE: All-purpose Lightweight Individual Carrying Equipment

APECS: All-Purpose Environmental Clothing System

ATPIAL: AN/PEQ-15 Advanced Target Pointer/Illuminator/Aiming Light

BDU: Battle Dress Uniform (Army term)

BLPS: Ballistic/Laser Protective Spectacles

CAP-ILBE (or CAP): ILBE Corpsman Assault Pack

CBIS: Chemical/Biological Individual Sampler

CBRN: chemical, biological, radiological and nuclear threats and protective equipment

CIF: Consolidated Issue Facility

COTS: commercial, off-the-shelf

CQBP: M45 Close Quarter Battle Pistol

DCU: Desert Camouflage Uniform (Army term)

DMR: Designated Marksman Rifle

EBNS: Enhanced Bed Net System

ECWCS: Extended Cold Weather Clothing System

ECWSS: Extended Cold Weather Sleeping System

EGA: Eagle, Globe and Anchor emblem

EMR: M39 Enhanced Marksman Rifle

EOD: Explosive Ordnance Disposal

ESAPI: Enhanced Small Arms Protective Inserts

FFME: Family of Field Medical Equipment

FILBE: Family of Improved Load-Bearing Equipment

FLC: Fighting Load Carrier

FR: flame-resistant

FROG: Flame-Resistant Organizational Gear (flame-resistant clothing)

FSBE: Full-Spectrum Battle Equipment

HE: high-explosive

HFR: AN/PRC-150 High-Frequency Radio

HHF: Handheld Flashlight

HHWS: Handheld Weather Station

IAR: M27 Infantry Automatic Rifle

IBA: Interceptor Body Armor

IBNS: Improved Bed Netting System

ICE: Infantry Combat Equipment

IED: Improvised Explosive Device

IFAK: Individual First Aid Kit

IIF: Individual Issue Facility

IIFS: Integrated Individual Fighting System

IISR: Integrated Intra-Squad Radio

IISR-HPH: Integrated Intra-Squad Radio Hearing Protection Headset

ILBE: Improved Load-Bearing Equipment

IMTV: Improved Modular Tactical Vest

IPIM: AN/PEQ-16 Integrated Pointer/Illuminator Module

ITLBV: IIFS Individual Tactical Load-Bearing Vest

ITPIAL: Infrared Target Pointer/Illuminator/Aiming Light

IWPS: Individual Water Purification System

JBPDS: Joint Biological Point Detection System

JCAD: Joint Chemical Agent Detector

JNLWP: Joint Non-Lethal Weapons Program

JSCS: Joint Service Combat Shotgun

JSLIST: Joint Service Lightweight Integrated Suit Technology (a CBRN protective suit)

JTRS: Joint Tactical Radio System

LAW: M72 series Light Anti-armor Weapon

LBE: Load-Bearing Equipment

LP-NVG: Low-Profile Night Vision Goggles

LRTI: Long Range Thermal Imager

LWH: Lightweight Helmet

MACK: Marine Assault Climber's Kit

MACS Sack: Marine Corps Stuff Sack

MAGTF: Marine Air-Ground Task Force

MARPAT: Marine Pattern digital camouflage

MARSOC: Marine Corps Forces Special Operations Command

MBITR: AN/PRC-148 Multiband Inter/Intra-Team Radio

MBK: Mechanical Breacher's Kit

MBR: AN/PRC-117 Multi-Band Radio

MCCB HW/TW: Marine Corps Combat Boot, Hot Weather and Temperate Weather versions

MCCDC: Marine Corps Combat Development Command

MCCUU: Marine Corps Combat Utility Uniform

MCCWIK: Marine Corps Cold Weather Infantry Kit

MCSC: Marine Corps Systems Command

MCWCS: Mountain Cold Weather Clothing System

MCWL: Marine Corps Warfighting Laboratory

MDO: Machine gun Day Optic

MEB: Marine Expeditionary Brigade

MEF: Marine Expeditionary Force

MEP: Marine Enhancement Program

MEPS: Military Eye Protection Systems

MERS: Marine Expeditionary Rifle Squad program

MEU: Marine Expeditionary Unit, usually

MEU (SOC) for "Special Operations Capable"

MNVD: Monocular Night Vision Device

MOLLE and **MOLLE II:** Modular Lightweight Load-Carrying Equipment

MOPP: Mission-Oriented Protective Posture (refers to level of CBRN protection)

MOUT: Military Operations on Urban Terrain

MRTB: Medium Range Thermal Bi-ocular

MSGL: M32 Multi-Shot Grenade Launcher

MSS: Modular Sleep System

MSTS: Modular Steel Traction Snowshoe

MTP: Multi-Terrain Pattern, a British camouflage pattern

MTI: Mini Thermal Imager

MTV: Modular Tactical Vest

MWS: Modular Weapon System

NLW: Non-Lethal Weapons

NVG: Night Vision Goggles

ONR: Office of Naval Research

OTV: Outer Tactical Vest

PALS: Pouch Attachment Ladder System

PASGT: Personnel Armor System, Ground Troops (body armor vest and helmet)

PC: USMC Plate Carrier (body armor vest)

POG: (pelvic) Protective Overgarment

PPE: Personal Protective Equipment

PPS: Pelvic Protection System

PRR: A/N PRC-343(V)1 (H4655) Personal Role Radio

PSR: Precision Sniper Rifle

PUGz: (pelvic) Protective Undergarment

RAS: Rail Adapter System

RAT: Rugged All-Terrain boot

RCO: Rifle Combat Optic

R-ILBE or **RILBE:** Reconnaissance ILBE pack system

SAPI: Small Arms Protective Insert

SASS: M110 Semi-Automatic Sniper System

SASR: M82 and M107 Special Application Scoped Rifle

SAW: M249 Squad Automatic Weapon

SDO: Squad Day Optic

S-ILBE or **SILBE:** Standard ILBE pack system

SINCGARS: AN/PRC-119 Single Channel Ground and Airborne Radio System

SMAW: Shoulder-launched Multipurpose Assault Weapon

SPC: Scalable Plate Carrier (body armor vest)

SPECS: Special Protective Eyewear, Cylindrical System

SPR: Mk 12 Special Purpose Rifle

SRAW: FGM-172 Predator Short-Range Assault Weapon

S-SAPI: Side Small Arms Protective Insert

SSDS: Scout Sniper Day Scope

SSMRNS: Scout Sniper Medium Range Night Sight

STAP: Special Training Allowance Pool

SWDG: Sun/Wind/Dust Goggles

THHR: Tactical Handheld Radio

TOW: Tube-Launched, Optically-Tracked, Wire-Guided Missile

TPIAL: Target Pointer/Illuminator/Aiming Light

UHIMIS: Ultra-High-Intensity Illumination System

UIF: Unit Issue Facility

USON: Urgent Statement of Need

UUNS: Urgent Universal Need Statement

WBI: ILBE Waterproofing Bag Insert

VLI: Visible Light Illuminator

VLIR: VLI Replacement

INDEX

Figures in **bold** refer to illustrations. Plates are shown with page locators in brackets.

air crews/aviators 6, 18, **20**, 28
anti-terrorist personnel 42, 54
assault/teams 5, 26, **D2(27)**
attachment rails: RAS (Mil-Std-1913) 30, **E2(31)**, 51–2, **52**, 54, 56, 59
automatic riflemen 10, **24**, 54, **H4(55)**, 57

bandoliers 14, **B10(15)**, 41, 46, 59
battalion landing teams **21**, 54, **56**
bayonets: M7 30, 51; OKC-3S/MPB 30, **E11(31)**, 51
belts: utility 14, **B1(15)**, 17, 40, 41, 60; waist 10, **A3(11)**, 14, **B7–8(15)**, 38, 40, 41; web 17
bivouac items 46: shelters: EBNS/IBNS 46; sleep-system carriers 14, **B8(15)**, 40, 44; sleeping bags/mats 23, 39, **42**, 46, 54, **H3–4(55)**: 3S/MSS 46; tarps 46; tents 23
body armor (armored vests) 8, **9**, 9, 12, **12**, 16, 17, 20, 22, 25, 26, 28–30, 32–3, 40, 44, 45, **45**, 46, **G7(47)**, 62: APES 28; ESAPI 29, **29**, 42, **F2(43)**; GTVBA 28; IMTV 32, **34**; Interceptor OTV 18, **C1**, 3**(19)**, 26, **26**, **D1–2(27)**, 28–30, **28**, 29, 32, **32**, 40, 40, 44, 46, 54, **H2–4(55)**; ISPC 32; MTV 29–30, 32, **32**, 35, 42, **F2(43)**, 44, **44**, 46, **G7(47)**; PASGT 10, **A2(11)**, 18, 25, 26, 29; PC 32, **33**, 34; PPS 17, 33; Quadgard 28; SAPI 18, **C1(19)**, 28, 29; SPC 32, **33**, 34, 42, **F1(43)**, 44, 45, 54, **H1(55)**; S-SAPI 28, 29

camouflage colors/patterns 7, **13**, 14, 16–17, **34**: Coyote Brown 498 16, 18, **C5(19)**, **23**, 24, 29, **34**, 41; Desert (3-col) 13–14, **13**, 16, 17; Desert (6-col "chocolate chip") 10, **A1(11)**, 13, 13, 14, 17; "digital" CADPAT 14; DPM MultiCam 16; light sand 24; MTP 16–17; Woodland 10, **A2(11)**, 13, **13**, 16, 17, 22, 25, 29, 34, 46
camouflage MARPATs 7, 14, 16, 17, 20: Desert **13**, 16, 17, 20, 23, 24, 26, **D1(27)**, 34, 60; Snow 16, **16**, 23, **24**, 54, **H4(55)**; Woodland **12**, 13, 16, 17, 20, 22, **23**, 41, 46
canteens (1 qt) 14, **B1(15)**, 18, **C10(19)**, 39, 40, 41, 44
carbines 42, 52, 57: M4 MWS 26, **D3(27)**, 51, 52, 57, 58; M4A1 52
cargo sleds 48, 54, **H2(55)**
CBRN clothing/equipment 12, 13, 18, **C3(19)**, 26, 37, **37**, 38, 48
cold weather clothing/equipment 12, 21, 22–3, 24, **24**, 25: APECS 22, 23, **23**, 24, 54, **H1–4(55)**; ECWCS 20–2, 23, 54, **H2(55)**; Gen II ECWCS 21–2, 24; Gen III ECWCS 22; MCCWIK 48; MCWCS 22–4, **23**, 24
combat engineers 28
combat knives: Mark 2 (KA-BAR) 18, **C1(19)**, 30, 40, 41, 51
combat logistics battalions/groups 6, 26, **D1(27)**, **32**, 35, 58
commercial items, approval/purchase of 10, 13, 23, 26, **D3(27)**, 35, 36, **36**, 42, 45, 46, 48, 54, **H1(55)**
corpsmen (medical personnel) 10, **A3(11)**, 40, 42, **42**, 45, 46, **G7(47)**
counter-insurgency operations 5, 6, 61–2

designated marksmen 30, **E12(31)**, 52, 53–4, **H1(55)**, 57

EOD personnel 53, 54
eye protection (eyewear) 10, 35–6

fire (support) teams **39**, 48, 54, **H2–3(55)**, 59
flame-resistant clothing (FROG) 7, 10, 12, 17, 18, 20, **20**, 21, 24, 26, **D3(27)**, 46, **G7(47)**, 54, **H4(55)**

flight suits 26, **D3(27)**
footwear 17–18: booties 23; boots 17, 18, 24, 37, 54, **H1**, 4**(55)**; overboots 18, **C3(19)**; snowshoes 48, 54, **H2**, 4**(55)**; socks 21
gas masks 37, 40: M40 18, **C4(19)**, 37, 38; M50 JSGPM 37, 38, **38**
grenade launchers 30, **E2(31)**, 58–9: M32/M32A1 MSGL 30, **E5(31)**, 58–9, **58**; M79 58; M203 18, **C3(19)**, 57, 58; Mk 19 AGL 59
grenades 18, **C10(19)**, 38, 57–8: CS/tear gas 58, 62; frag: M67 42, **F3(43)**, 44, 54, **H1(55)**, 57; HE 18, **C6–7(19)**, 40, 42, **F3(43)**, 44, 58; incendiary 44: AN-M14 TH3 58; offensive concussion: Mk 3A2 57–8; pyrotechnic 18, **C5(19)**, 40; smoke 42, **F3(43)**, 44: AN-M8 HC 58; M18 58; star cluster 44; (stun/"flash-bang") 44, 62: M84 58; white phosphorus: M15 58
grenadiers 10, 39, 40

handwear 23: gloves 18, **C3(19)**, 20, 21, 23, 24, 26, **D3(27)**, 37; mittens 21, 23
headwear 10, 23, 25: balaclavas 20; caps **12**, 17, 23, 25; helmet covers **10**, 23, **24**, 34, 54; helmets 18, **C3(19)**, 21, 25, **25**, 33–5, 48, 62: ACH **35**, 54, **H1(55)**; ECH 34, 35; LWH 8, 26, **D2(27)**, 34, **34**, 35, 46, **G7(47)**; PASGT 10, **A2(11)**, 33–4
health protection officers 37
hearing protection (noise attenuation) 36–7, 50
hydration bladders/systems (3 ltr/100oz) 14, **B6(15)**, 39, 40, 41, 42, **F7–7a(43)**, 44, **44**, 45, 46, **G1**, 3**(47)**

insignia/badges 7, **7**, 8, **9**, 13, 16, 17, 25, **25**

joint protection 35

landing units 25, **25**
legwear: gaiters 24, 54, **H4(55)**
load-bearing equipment 8–9, 10, 12, 22: ALC 44; ALICE 10, **A2(11)**, 14, **B1–2(15)**, 38, 39, 40; Chest Rig **45**; FILBE **35**, 45, 46, **G1–6(47)**; FLC 18, **C10(19)**, 41, 44; FSBE 42; IIF 40; IIFS 10, **A1(11)**, 14, 25, 38–9; ILBE 18, **21**, 41–2, 42, **F3–6**, 8–10**(43)**, 44, 44, 45, 46, **G5**, 7**(47)**; ITLBV 39, 40; LBV 10, **A3(11)**, 14, **B1(15)**, 18, 38–9, 40, 41, 54, **H3(55)**; MOLLE 10, **A3(11)**, 14, **B1–2**, 8, 12**(15)**, 18, **C2**, 5–11**(19)**, 26, **D1(27)**, 29, 39–41, 39, 40, 42, 44, 45, 54, **H2(55)**; MOLLE II 10, 18, **C8–9(19)**, 41

machine gun teams 54
machine gunners 10, **A2(11)**
machine guns 46: heavy: M2 56; light: M249 SAW 54, 56; medium: M240 10, **A2(11)**, 30, **E13(31)**, 54, 56, 57
magazines 14, **B1**, 3–5, 10**(15)**, 18, **C8–10(19)**, 38, 39, **39**, 40, 41, 42, **F3–6(43)**, 44, 45, **G5(47)**, 54, **H1(55)**
medical kits: IFAK 10, 14, **B1(15)**, 18, **C1**, 10**(19)**, 40, 41, 42, **F3(43)**, 45, 46
mortar teams **60**; mortars 28: 60mm M224 8, 60, 61; 81mm M252/252A1 **60**, 61

night vision devices 14, 36, 51: flashlights 57; goggles 10, **A2(11)**, 48, 49; image intensifiers 48, 56, 57; lasers 57; monocles 48–9; spectacles 36; thermal imagers 48–9, 56, 57

optics (field) 46, **52**: M22/M24/M49/TIF 48

pads (knee/elbow) 17, 35, **36**
paracord bracelets 46, **G7(47)**
pistol holsters 35, 45, 46, **G5(47)**
pistols 14, 35, 40, 42, **F5(43)**, 44, 46, **G5(47)**: M9/

M9A1 10, **A1–2(11)**, 30, **E3(31)**, 45, 51, 52, **54**, 57; M45 45, 51; M1911 51

radios 8, 9, 14, **B9(15)**, 37, 41, 42, **F9(43)**, 49, 50–1, 62: AN/PRC-117 50; AN/PRC-119 SINCGARS 41, 50; AN/PRC-126 IISR 49; AN/PRC-148 MBITR 26, **D3a(27)**, 50; AN/PRC-150 HFR 50–1; AN/PRC-152 50; AN/PRC-153 50; AN/PRC-343(V)1 IISR 50, 50; AN/RC-104 51; H4855 PRR 50, 50; HRFS 49; JTRS 49, 50; THHR 50
recon teams/troops 42, 51, 52, 56
rifle companies/squads 53, 59, 62
riflemen 10, 18, **C10(19)**, 39, 40
rifles 12, 38, 44, 45, 52, 57: DMR 53, 57; M14 52, 53; M16 family 14, **B10(15)**, 18, **C3**, **10(19)**, 26, **D1(27)**, 30, **E2(31)**, 40, 41, 42, **F3(43)**, 44, 46, **G7(47)**, 51, 52, 53, 54, 54, **H2**, 4**(55)**, 56, 57, 58; M27 IAR 30, **E4(31)**, 52, 54, 56, 57; M39 EMR 30, **E12(31)**, 53–4; M82A3 SASR 53, 57; M107 SASR 53; M110 53–4; M203 MWS 30, **E2(31)**, 42; M249 10; Mk 12 Mod 1 SPR 53, 54, **H1(55)**; Remington 700 52; SAM-R 53
rocket/missile launchers 59–61, **59**: FGM-148 Javelin 60; FGM-172 Predator SRAW 60–1; FIM-92 Stinger 61; M-47 Dragon 60; M72 LAW 9, 30, **E7(31)**, 59, **59**; M136 30, **E6(31)**, 54, 59; Mk 153 SMAW 26, **D2(27)**, 59–60; TOW 2/2B ATWS-H 61

sappers (de-mining operations) **20**
scopes/sights 51, 56–7: ACOG 57; AN/PVQ-31 series RCO 26, **D3(27)**, 30, **E2(31)**, 46, **G7(47)**, 56, 57; AN/PVS-4 57; AN/PVS-10 30, **E12(31)**, 57; AN/PVS-14 48; AN/PVS-27 SSMRNS 57; HDS 57; Leupold M 57; M145 30, **E10(31)**, 57; M68 CCO 56, 57; RX01 57; SSDS 57; SU-258/PVQ SDO 30, **E4(31)**, 57; SU-260P MDO 30, **E13(31)**, 57; TS-30 series 54, **H1(55)**, 57; Unertl 57
scout snipers 48, 52–3, **52**, 53, 57
scouts **29**; security personnel 33, 54
shotguns 5, 42, **F6(43)**, 44, 46, 52: Beneli M1014 JSCS 30, **E1(31)**, 52; Mossberg 500A1/A2 52; Remington 870 52
sniper rifles 53: M40 52–3; M110 SASS 53; Mk 11 Mod 1 53; PSR 53
snipers/sniper teams **29**, 46, 52, 57
special operations forces (SOC) 6, 7, 16–17, 22, 26, 28, 42, 51, 52, 56
special-purpose items/kits: 12, 46, 48: MACK 48; MBK 46, 48; MCCWIK 48
squad automatic weapons 40, 44, 57: M27 IAR 30, 54; M249 SAW 30, **E10(31)**, 40, 42, **F4(43)**, 54, **H4(55)**, 54
squad leaders 18, **C3(19)**, 45, 58

target designators, laser: AN/PEQ-2/-2A TTPIAL 26, **D3(27)**, 57; AN/PEQ-15 56; AN/PEQ-16/-16A 30, **E13(31)**, 54, **H1(55)**; AN/PSQ-18 30, **E2(31)**
target illuminators: flares 42, **F3(43)**, 44, 58; flashlights 30, 46, **G7(47)**, 51, 52, 56; MX-991/U 49; HHF 49; UHIMIS 49; VLI/VLIR 57; lasers 51, 56, 62: AN/PEQ-15 46, **G7(47)**
tools **C11(19)**, 41, 44, 46, **46**, 48, 54, **H1(55)**

uniforms 8, 10, **10**, **A1–2(11)**, 12, **12**, 17, 18, 20, **20**, 25, **34**, 35, **60**

weapons crews/platoons 26, **D2(27)**, 51, 53
webbing 14, **B1(15)**: PALS 14, **B1(15)**, 29, 32, 39–40, 42, 44, 45, 46